The Ypsilanti Preschool Curriculum Demonstration Project was made possible by a grant from the federal government under Title III of the Elementary and Secondary Education Act through the Ypsilanti Public School System, Ypsilanti, Michigan. Funds granted by the Spencer Foundation of Chicago and the Carnegie Corporation of New York made it possible to undertake follow-up data collection, data analysis, and preparation of the final report. The statements made and views expressed are solely the responsibility of the authors.

HIGH/SCOPE
EDUCATIONAL RESEARCH FOUNDATION
Ypsilanti, Michigan

Monographs of the
High/Scope Educational Research Foundation
Number Four

# THE YPSILANTI PRESCHOOL CURRICULUM DEMONSTRATION PROJECT
## Preschool Years and Longitudinal Results

D.P. Weikart, A.S. Epstein,
L. Schweinhart and J.T. Bond
High/Scope Educational Research Foundation

*with commentary by*
J. McV. Hunt
University of Illinois

**Library of Congress Cataloging in Publication Data**

Main entry under title:

The Ypsilanti preschool curriculum demonstration project.

   (Monographs of the High/Scope Educational Research Foundation; no. 4   ISSN 0149-242X)
   Bibliography: p.
   1. Education, Preschool—Michigan—Ypsilanti—Curricula. I. Weikart, David P. II. Series: High/Scope Educational Research Foundation. Monographs of the High/Scope Educational Research Foundation; no. 4.
LB 1140.2.Y69    372.21    77-92917

ISBN 0-931114-03-9

# Contents

# Tables & Figures

## Tables

**Tables** (continued)

# Figures

# Preface

The Ypsilanti Preschool Curriculum Demonstration Project is the second in a series of preschool intervention projects exploring the potential of early education for the long-term development of children. The first study, the Ypsilanti Perry Preschool Project, examined the impact of preschool attendance on school performance with the goal of reducing school dropout rates and juvenile delinquency. The basic findings from that project after 15 years of longitudinal study of the 123 participating children indicate that (1) experimental-group children significantly out-score control-group children on standardized achievement tests at eighth grade, nine years after the end of the program; and (2) experimental-group children are significantly *less* likely to have been retained in grade or placed in special education programs throughout their elementary-school years than children in the control group. In addition, an economic analysis of the Perry Project shows that the total cost of the project was more than recovered, primarily from savings which resulted because students with preschool required less costly forms of education as they progressed through elementary school. The question whether the ability to cope more successfully with the demands of the public schools will extend into the children's adolescence and adulthood is currently being investigated.

In 1967, when planning for the Curriculum Demonstration Project began, these favorable findings from the Perry Project were only sug-gested by the data available at that time. The results from other early preschool studies were not encouraging. The intensive small-scale ex-perimental studies produced a pattern of immediate gains on most mea-sures employed relative to the control group. However, broad statewide and national studies were discouraging; positive results were difficult to obtain, and most projects reported that initially encouraging outcomes tended to disappear over time.

The well publicized failure of Head Start children to maintain their gains in the elementary-school years was interpreted as a failure of the schools to capitalize on the abilities the children had developed in pre-school. As a result, National Follow Through was initiated in 1967; curriculum-model sponsors were added in 1968 to assist a number of school systems in developing the necessary alternatives to their regular program to facilitate the growth of Head Start graduates. A number of psychologists and educators also began to provide services to families in their homes instead of in group settings.

A further response by some researchers and most educators to the "failure" of preschool education was that the instruments available to assess preschool children and programs were too limited in scope. While excellent standardized measures existed for aptitude assessment, achievement tests were limited to those reflecting the regular school curriculum. Sensitive measures of important capacities such as self-concept, inquisitiveness, independence, initiative, etc. were all but nonexistent.

Many researchers noted that the programs which were most effective were those which espoused a structured curriculum. A structured curriculum has been interpreted by most educators to mean a didactic program with instructional "cookbooks" to aid teachers in remediating the difficulties learners encounter. It is possible, however, to have a "structured" program without directive instruction. Such programs as High/Scope's Cognitively Oriented Curriculum require the teacher to work within a system of education based on a specific child-development theory—a "structure," but one in which the initiative of both teacher and child are of paramount importance.

The Ypsilanti Preschool Curriculum Demonstration Project was established to explore the basic question posed by the findings on curriculum structure: If preschool education is an effective way of helping disadvantaged children to be successful in school (and the answer to that question from the perspective of the longitudinal findings of the Perry Project is a definite yes), then of all the theoretically diverse systems of preschool education, which one is most effective? It has taken almost a decade to arrive at a point where some answers to this question can be reviewed. That is the purpose of this monograph.

Like the Perry Project, the Ypsilanti Preschool Curriculum Demonstration Project is a longitudinal effort requiring the commitment and dedication of staff for an extended period of time. Because the project involved more than one curriculum theory, individuals outside of the project staff were involved to assure the quality of the two curricula not developed by High/Scope staff members. Of special note were the staff of Siegfried Engelmann at the University of Illinois; C. Bruner and Jean Osborn provided onsite direction and assisted in our efforts to replicate the spirit and conditions of what is now known as the DISTAR system in our Language Curriculum. The teachers in the Language Program over the years of the project were Bettye McDonald, Susan Lovejoy, Jackie Bree, Linda Hiatt, and Sheila Mainwaring. Based on the Perry Project, the Cognitively Oriented Curriculum was maintained by Donna McClelland (who also served as general supervisor to the entire classroom component of the project), Linda Rogers, and Pat Nederveld. The classroom teachers included Rose Tapp, Pat Nederveld, Mary Ann Smith, and Jean Kluge. The Unit-Based Curriculum was developed by Mary Lou Malte and Mary Martin, who evolved their program over the entire three years of the project.

The research for the project was conducted by many dedicated individuals who maintained the quality and accuracy of the data. Specifically Martin Heilweil, Robert Rentfrow, Kelvin Seifert, Fariyal Sheriff, Donald Sommerfeld, Ronald Wiegerink, Dennis Deloria, John Larson, and Sarah Lawser, as well as many part-time testers, were involved. The report presented here had additional assistance from Pamela Schwartz, Judy McNeil, Robert Hanvey, Nancy Naylor, Mary Hohmann, Jana Grimston, and Cathy Peterson. Lynn Spencer edited the report.

As with any long-term study of this nature, assistance from the teachers, administrative staff, and Board of Education of the Ypsilanti Public Schools and several surrounding school districts has been essential for the success of this study. Without their assistance and at times personal sacrifice, the project would not have survived the rigors of time and change. Finally, the parents and the children themselves have repeatedly cooperated in the project, making them the authors of this work. Without the active assistance of all of these individuals and institutions this project would never have been carried through to completion.

David P. Weikart
Ypsilanti, Michigan
November 1977

# I Background

# ORIGINS OF THE PROJECT

The Curriculum Demonstration Project grew out of the Ypsilanti Perry Preschool Project, which was operated by the Ypsilanti, Michigan, Public School System from fall 1962 through spring 1967 under the direction of David P. Weikart. The main purpose of the Perry Project was to determine whether a cognitively oriented preschool program could help economically disadvantaged children to be more successful in school. Two eligibility criteria were employed. First, children's families had to be in the lowest income group within the predominantly low-income Perry Elementary School attendance area and, second, each child had to be certified by school psychologists as "educable mentally retarded" according to existing State of Michigan special education regulations (IQ below 85 with no indication of organic causes and no major physical handicaps).

Over the course of the project, 123 children participated, entering the project in five successive "waves" one year apart. Approximately equal numbers of children in each wave were assigned to independent experimental and control groups. Experimental-group children attended half-day preschool for two years, and they and their mothers received home visits from preschool teachers every week during the school year. The only intervention that control-group children received was annual testing. The educational program which evolved[1] over this five-year period focused on cognitive-developmental goals, drawing heavily upon Jean Piaget's theory of mental development.

By 1967, it was evident that the educational approach taken in the Perry Project could substantially increase three- and four-year-old children's level of performance on standardized tests of cognitive-linguistic ability which typically predict school success. Moreover, preliminary follow-up data on the public-school experience of older children in the sample indicated that children who had attended preschool were scoring higher on tests of academic achievement than children who had not attended preschool (Weikart, 1967). In short, the program seemed to be effective.

During this same period, other approaches to compensatory preschool education were being developed, implemented, and evaluated by other research groups. Results from these studies suggested that not all preschool programs were equally effective for economically disadvantaged children. But the reasons for their differential effectiveness were not discernible because major discrepancies in research designs did not permit direct comparisons of findings.

The Ypsilanti Preschool Curriculum Demonstration Project (hereafter referred to as the CD Project) was designed to address the question whether some approaches to compensatory preschool education for economically disadvantaged children were more effective than others under controlled experimental conditions. The CD Project examined the

---

[1]The curriculum model of the Perry Project is described in Weikart et al. (1970). A more recent description of the High/Scope Educational Research Foundation's curriculum, reflecting 15 years of development, can be found in Hohmann et al. (1978).

effects of three preschool curriculum models on children's cognitive, linguistic, socio-emotional and academic skills development while holding noncurriculum factors as constant as possible across the programs being compared. Measurement of the development of these various skills focused on both concurrent gains and longitudinal assessment during elementary school through grade 4. The programs selected for comparison represented major, and in some degree competing, approaches to early childhood education. The experimental programs were in operation from fall 1967 through spring 1970.[2]

# THE CURRICULUM MODELS

When the CD Project was conceptualized, there were numerous well publicized approaches to early childhood education already in operation and many more programs in the early stages of development. Observations of classroom processes in diverse programs, however, suggested that there were three basic curriculum models for preschool education (Weikart, 1972; see figure 1):

**Programmed.** In this model, the typical role of the teacher is to initiate learning activities, and the role of the child is to respond to what the teacher offers. These curricula have clearly defined objectives, incorporate carefully designed programmed sequences to move children toward these objectives, and provide teachers with explicit instructions for implementing learning sequences. Content usually emphasizes specific pre-academic skills. Learning is viewed as the acquisition of "correct" responses with respect to programmed goals. It is assumed that virtually anything can be taught to almost any child, through the use of behavior-modification techniques, if behavioral objectives are specific enough.

**Open Framework.** In this model, both teacher and child initiate learning activities. The primary educational objective for the child is the development of fundamental cognitive processes and concepts, rather than specific skills (although it is assumed that specific skills will be acquired in the course of general development). Cognitive development is viewed as the product of the child's direct experience in and action upon his environment. The curriculum is generally derived from an explicit theory of child development which provides a decision-making framework for teachers without specifying the day-to-day content of the program. Learning occurs through the child's active and largely intrinsically motivated involvement in an environment structured by the teacher.

---

[2]The experimental programs were operated under the auspices of the Ypsilanti, Michigan Public School System. In 1970, David P. Weikart, director of the Project, left the Ypsilanti Public School System and with his staff formed the High/Scope Educational Research Foundation, a private, nonprofit educational research and development organization located in Ypsilanti. Longitudinal follow-up of children who participated in the three preschool programs has been conducted by the High/Scope Educational Research Foundation.

**Figure 1**

*Preschool Curriculum Models*

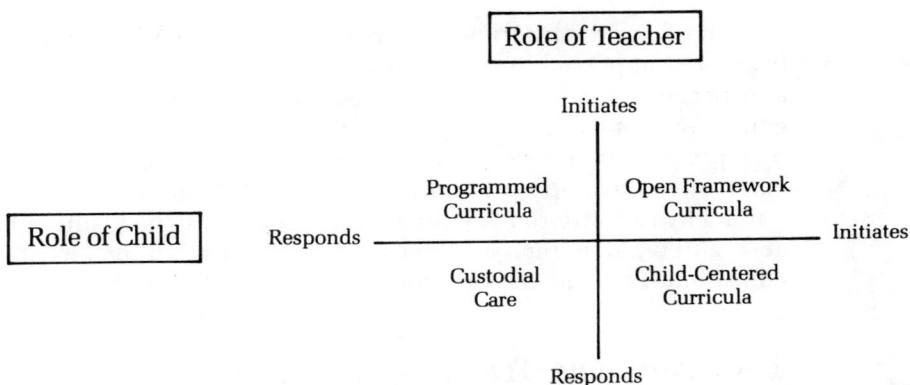

```
                                    ┌─────────────────┐
                                    │ Role of Teacher │
                                    └─────────────────┘

                                         Initiates
                                            │
                Programmed        │        Open Framework
                 Curricula        │          Curricula
┌──────────────┐                  │
│ Role of Child│  Responds ───────┼───────────────────── Initiates
└──────────────┘                  │
                 Custodial        │        Child-Centered
                   Care           │           Curricula
                                            │
                                         Responds
```

**Child-Centered.**   In this model, the child typically initiates learning while the teacher responds to the child's particular interests and activities. The great majority of preschool programs are in this category. They are characterized by a focus on the development of the "whole" child, emphasizing social and emotional growth and self-expression rather than the acquisition of specific pre-academic skills or cognitive development. Classroom environments are typically open and ideally stimulus-rich. The relationship between teacher and child tends to be permissive. Content revolves around things of interest to the child which support his general socialization-enculturation, providing opportunities for independent and creative activity and the exploration and development of healthy peer relationships.

Although this taxonomy admittedly oversimplifies reality, it seems to reflect important differences in actual preschool programs. Interestingly, Kohlberg and Mayer (1972) seem to have identified the same three approaches in an analysis of the evolution of Western educational ideologies. Using their terminology, Programmed Curricula seem to derive from cultural transmission ideology and associationistic-learning theory; Open Framework Curricula, from progressive ideology and cognitive developmental theory; and Child-Centered Curricula, from romantic ideology and maturationist theory. Each of the three curricula selected for comparison in the CD Project represented one of these approaches:

**The Language Training Curriculum**—a programmed (cultural transmission, associationistic-learning) approach based on the Bereiter and Engelmann (1966) program developed at the University of Illinois

**The Cognitively Oriented Curriculum**—an open framework (progressive, cognitive developmental) approach developed during the Ypsilanti Perry Preschool Project and extended by the High/Scope Educational Research Foundation

**The Unit-Based Curriculum**—a child-centered (romantic, maturationist) approach, modeled after traditional nursery school programs which focus on the social and emotional growth of the child

The Cognitively Oriented Curriculum was incorporated in the design because it appeared to represent a major alternative to other approaches and because Ypsilanti Public School staff involved in early childhood education wanted to assess the relative strengths and weaknesses of their own program in order to make rational decisions about the future of their curriculum development efforts. Selection of the other two programs was guided by two criteria: any program chosen had to be readily implementable, and it had to represent one of the three distinct models of preschool education. Brief descriptions of each program follow.[3]

## The Language Training Curriculum[4]

The Language Training Curriculum was adapted from the work of Bereiter and Engelmann at the University of Illinois. Their book, *Teaching Disadvantaged Children in Preschool* (1966), was the primary theoretical resource for this programmed model. Bereiter and Engelmann designed their approach specifically to help economically disadvantaged children succeed in school. Their compensatory strategy was to maximize children's acquisition of specific pre-academic skills through direct, programmed instruction. The program was also intended (1) to improve children's self-confidence and self-image by providing opportunities for academic success in an atmosphere of friendly competition, and (2) to produce well socialized students by bringing these children's social behavior in the preschool classroom under the control of reinforcement contingencies common to elementary school.

The academic problems of economically disadvantaged children were viewed as stemming mostly from inadequate language development. The authors argued that while these children were capable of communicating and understanding desires and commands, they were much less able to use language as a means of communicating information than their middle-class peers. Specifically, it was observed that disadvantaged children tended to talk in phrases rather than complete sentences and to use "giant words" (i.e., phrases which are used as single units of speech and cannot be readily broken down and recombined into new constructions). These inflexible verbal codes were, in turn, assumed to severely restrict the children's ability to cope with the academic demands of school, which are expressed and satisfied for the most part in linguistic modes.

The preschool day was divided into six periods:

(1) *Unstructured time* (20 minutes)—children play with materials of their own choice (puzzles, small blocks, table games, etc.).

---

[3]A 16mm color film entitled "This Is the Way We Go to School," produced by the High/Scope Educational Research Foundation, depicts each of the three models and presents the basic research findings of the CD Project.

[4]The Language Training Curriculum as implemented in the CD Project is described by McClelland et al. (1970).

(2) *Group singing* (15 minutes)—children learn songs and sing them under the direction of teachers.

(3) *Structured time* (60 minutes, 20 minutes for each of three content areas)—children are instructed in language, reading, and arithmetic, in small groups.

(4) *Semi-structured time* (20 minutes)—children are taught diverse school-related skills such as coloring, cutting, pasting, sharing of materials, group games.

(5) *Juice time* (15 minutes)—children have a snack and rest.

(6) *Story time* (10 minutes)—children listen to a story read by the teacher and answer questions about it which focus on current instructional goals.

An additional 10 minutes or so were spent in "settling in" at the beginning of the day and dismissal at the end of the day.

The core of the educational program was "structured time" during which children received programmed instruction in three content areas:

**Language.** This component of the educational program focused on the structural and logical components of spoken standard English. A primary objective was that children learn the "substitution property" of language—that language has discrete parts which can be related, rearranged, and interchanged according to certain rules. Specific activities emphasized labeling, words as basic units, negation, polar opposites, compounds, plurals, prepositions, pronouns, if-then statements, verb tense, and speaking in complete sentences.

**Reading.** Reading was approached in the same systematic, analytic way as language. Emphasis was placed on phonetic skills, which permit one to pronounce what is written. Children were taught to produce the phonemes of standard English and to recognize them in written language.

**Arithmetic.** Arithmetic, too, was treated as an essentially linguistic phenomenon in which numbers are the basic units, and rules of ordination and computation constitute a grammar. Instruction focused initially on rote learning of numbers, then on identifying written numerals and on rules for relating numbers (seriation and computation). By the end of preschool, children were expected to have acquired basic computational skills in addition and subtraction. This component of the educational program also emphasized recognition of "equality" (e.g., matching a series of picture cards set up by the teacher).

Instructional activities consisted largely of drills in which teachers modeled correct language and elicited imitative linguistic production by the children. (Manipulation of concrete materials and self-initiated learning did not play a significant role in the educational program.) Detailed instructional workbooks prepared by the authors of the curriculum became available shortly after the project began and provided teachers with standard materials to use with the children (Engelmann, Osborn and Engelmann, 1969; Engelmann and Bruner, 1969; Engelmann and Carnine,

1969). In each content area, learning activities were presented to the children in a programmed sequence, and learning goals were behaviorally explicit; only when children had mastered specific skills at one level in a sequence did they move on to more complex activities at a higher level. Children were divided into three groups (about five children in each) for instruction in each content area according to ability. One teacher or paraprofessional worked with each small group, covering the three content areas each day. Teacher expectations were geared to individual rates of development, thus guaranteeing high rates of success for most children.

Teachers relied primarily on positive reinforcements to shape and sustain desired behaviors in the children and achieve behavioral objectives. Initially, primary reinforcements (e.g., raisins) were used along with verbal and social reinforcements. Gradually primary reinforcements were entirely replaced by verbal and social reinforcements. Occasionally a child was punished for misbehaving by separating him from the rest of the class or by withholding juice and cookies.

## The Cognitive Curriculum[5]

The Cognitive Curriculum offered teachers (1) a conceptual model of child development within which children's day-to-day behavior made sense, and (2) a related set of educational goals and strategies which could be used to systematically plan and evaluate a developmental program for three- and four-year-old children. It was assumed that mental growth occurs through children's active exploration and manipulation of their environment and through transactions with their peers as well as with adults and adult language, rather than by rote learning. Teaching goals focused on basic intellective processes and cognitive structures which undergo important changes during the preschool years. Teaching strategies were designed to provide children with the experiential basis for achieving cognitive developmental goals. Within the framework created by the curriculum, children were encouraged to initiate and regulate their own learning.

More specifically, the curriculum identified "key experiences" through which the child's emerging mental abilities could be broadened and strengthened rather than accelerated or directly taught, and it offered general strategies which could help teachers provide these experiences. The key experiences included:

**Active learning**—direct exploration with all senses; discovering relationships through concrete experience; taking care of one's own needs; choosing materials, activities, purposes; etc.

**Planning and evaluating**—verbally articulating a plan; identifying the steps involved in carrying it out; comparing what was actually accomplished with one's original plan; etc.

---

[5]The Cognitively Oriented Curriculum, or the "Cognitive Curriculum" as it was called in the CD Project, is described in two volumes—McClelland et al. (1970) and Weikart et al. (1971). The cognitive-developmental theory of Jean Piaget provided the foundation for this "open framework" model.

**Using language**—conversing about meaningful experiences with adults and peers; describing objects, events, and relations; expressing feelings in words; having one's own spoken language written down and read back; listening to stories; telling stories; etc.

**Representing**—recognizing objects by sound, touch, taste, and smell only; imitating actions; relating pictures, photographs, and models to real places and things; role playing and pretending; drawing and painting; etc.

**Classification**—investigating and labeling the attributes of things; noticing and describing how things are the same and how they are different (sorting); describing something in several ways; etc.

**Seriation**—comparing things and their attributes; arranging several things in order along the same dimension and describing the relations matching one ordered set with another; etc.

**Number concepts**—comparing number and amount; exploring one-to-one correspondence; enumerating objects as well as counting by rote; etc.

**Temporal relations**—describing past events in words; anticipating future events verbally and by making appropriate preparations; describing the order of events; planning and completing what one has planned; using conventional time units; observing seasonal changes; etc.

**Spatial relations**—fitting things together and taking them apart; rearranging things in space; observing things and places from different spatial viewpoints; describing the position of things in relation to each other; interpreting representations of spatial relations in drawings and pictures; etc.

Strategies for providing children with these experiences included, among other things, procedures for arranging and equipping the classroom and for setting up a consistent routine and communicating it to the children; and ways to help children plan, carry out, and review their own activities. The classroom was organized into four work areas: large motor (blocks, trucks, climber, etc.); fine motor (puzzles, clay, etc.); housekeeping (stove, refrigerator, dolls, costumes, etc.); and art. The day was divided into eight periods, each of which provided opportunities for learning:

(1) *Planning time* (20 minutes)—children, assisted by adults, set daily activity goals for themselves.

(2) *Work time* (40 minutes)—children carry out plans in work areas.

(3) *Group time* (10 minutes)—self-evaluation and group discussion of work done; teacher-initiated activities centering on cognitive goals.

(4) *Cleanup* (15 minutes)—as children clean work areas, teachers help them classify and seriate the materials.

(5) *Juice time* (25 minutes)—teachers work informally on predetermined goals with small groups of children.

(6) *Activity time* (15 minutes)—teachers initiate group activities either indoors (music, games) or outdoors (games, use of playground equipment).

(7) *Circle time* (15 minutes)—teachers lead a review of the day's work and may read stories.

(8) *Dismissal* (10 minutes)—teachers introduce concepts experienced during the day into the process of preparing to go home.

The daily routine provided children with concrete experiences in temporal relations and was designed to help them master fundamental temporal concepts.

## The Unit-Based Curriculum[6]

The Unit-Based Curriculum grew out of the traditional nursery school approach to early childhood education. The general orientation of traditional nursery schools has been reviewed by Sears and Dowley (1963) and Swift (1964). The term "unit-based" refers to the teachers' use of content units or themes (e.g., holidays, farm animals, circus, seasons, etc.) as the foci of activities and discussions over the course of the year.

The Unit-Based Curriculum did not have an extensive theoretical basis. As in traditional nursery schools, teachers in the Unit-Based Program were guided in their day-to-day formulation of the educational program by their own intuition and by several general assumptions about child development:

- That children learn and develop by discovering for themselves, through direct experience, how the world works.
- That children are intrinsically motivated to learn about the world.
- That their intrinsic motivation to learn may be stifled, however, by a restrictive environment or by their own emotional insecurity.
- That different children have different needs, interests, and talents. They develop in different ways and at different rates. Consequently, there is no single most desirable developmental sequence or outcome.
- That social, emotional, physical, and aesthetic development are just as important as intellectual development to the well being of the whole child.
- That the optimal educational environment is one which is affectively warm, socially permissive, and experientially rich and which permits and encourages each child to chart his own course of development.

Given these assumptions, teachers were expected to exercise their own judgment in determining the specific needs of individual children. The resulting program was in the main child-centered—i.e., more responsive to children's needs and interests than expressive of predetermined

---

[6]The educational approach taken in the Unit-Based Program is described by McClelland et al. (1970).

objectives. This is not to suggest that the Unit-Based Program was without objectives. On the contrary, teachers viewed preschool as preparing children for kindergarten by helping them develop their attention span, interact positively with peers, acquire good manners, develop a positive self-concept, and acquire language and concepts which would be expected of them in kindergarten.

However, while middle-class children seemed to achieve these objectives without much intervention by teachers, economically disadvantaged children seemed to require substantial directive intervention by teachers. Consequently, the Unit-Based Program was somewhat more structured than traditional nursery school programs serving middle-class children.

The preschool day was divided into five parts:

(1) *Circle time and music time* (45 minutes)—teachers work with the entire group of children (usually seated), introducing unit-related materials, reading stories, singing songs, working with puppets, counting, learning body parts or one another's names.

(2) *Discovery time and cleanup* (60 minutes)—children engage in free play in one of four activity areas (housekeeping, large-motor, fine-motor, art).

(3) *Group time* (15 minutes)—teachers read stories or initiate relatively quiet activities (e.g., coloring, pasting) and children have juice and cookies.

(4) *Outdoor time* (15 minutes)—children engage in free play outdoors when weather permits.

(5) *Dismissal* (15 minutes)—children prepare to go home.

Within the context of this routine, teachers attempted to meet what they perceived to be the special needs of economically disadvantaged children:

- Teachers took care not to "overstimulate" the children with too rich an environment. They demonstrated how unfamiliar materials could be used and introduced additional materials gradually over the course of the year.

- Teachers tried to help children build more positive self-concepts by interacting with them individually during most of the day, encouraging them to learn and use each other's names, always rewarding individual creativity and "good" behavior with praise, accepting idiosyncratic behavior within broad limits of social propriety, and not confronting children with their failures and mistakes.

- Considerable attention was given to the development of "manners," prosocial values and behavior, and self-control. Teacher expectations in these domains were made explicit. Teachers tried to set examples and praised children when they behaved appropriately.

- Teachers emphasized language and concept development more than would have been the case had children come from middle-class homes. Throughout the day teachers conversed with children, encouraging and helping them to talk about needs, feelings, interests, ideas, and experiences, both with adults and with one another. In addition, during circle time and group time, teachers introduced activities designed to help children learn colors, shapes, numbers, body parts, object labels, and so forth.

Thus, while the Unit-Based Program resembled traditional programs, more teacher direction was evident than in most traditional nursery schools.

# HOME VISITS IN THE THREE PROGRAMS

In addition to the classroom programs, each child and mother received bi-weekly 90-minute home visits from one of the child's teachers. The activities which families and teachers engaged in during these home-teaching sessions were consistent with the curriculum model implemented in the child's classroom. These activities are detailed in chapter III.

The purpose of the home visits was to involve mothers in helping their children learn at home. Both the mother and the child were therefore expected to be present for the session. The emphasis on maternal participation was an outgrowth of the staff's prior experience in the Perry Project. They felt that parents became more involved in the educational process when they saw that their child's growth was enhanced by working with the teacher, rather than regarding the teacher as a "model" whose purpose was to "educate" the parent during the session.

Although only 1½ hours were spent in the home every two weeks, compared to 25 hours in the classroom, teachers felt that home visit sessions were an essential component of the programs. They valued both the intensive contact with the mother and the obviously "special" relationship they shared with the child in the one-to-one situation at home. CD Project staff hoped that by involving the mother in her child's education, an impact would be made upon the home environment. An educationally supportive home environment would not only facilitate the child's development during the preschool years, but would also provide the basis for continued growth in elementary school long after the program had ended.

# OTHER PRESCHOOL COMPARISON STUDIES

Several other major preschool comparison studies were being conducted at about the same time as the CD Project. All of these projects had a common interest in determining whether different preschool programs have different impacts on economically disadvantaged children. Brief descriptions of each project are presented in this section. Research findings of these studies will be considered in the final chapter of this report, where an attempt is made to integrate them with findings from the CD Project.

## Karnes research and development program

In 1965, Merle B. Karnes and her associates initiated a research project comparing five different preschool programs selected to represent varying degrees of structure—from relatively unstructured traditional nursery school models to a highly structured programmed instruction model (Karnes, 1969 and 1973). Children attended preschool for two hours, fifteen minutes a day, five days a week, during a single school year. Following preschool, children from the Traditional, Community-Integrated, and Montessori programs entered regular kindergarten. Children from the Bereiter-Engelmann program attended a special half-day kindergarten program, and children from Karnes' Ameliorative program participated in a special one-hour program each day in addition to regular kindergarten. Approximately 120 children participated in the five programs.

## Miller and Dyer experimental variation of Head Start curricula

In 1968, Louise B. Miller and Jean L. Dyer initiated a study to compare the effects of four preschool programs (Miller & Dyer, 1975). As in the Karnes study, programs were selected to represent a broad range of approaches to early childhood education: Traditional Head Start, Montessori, Darcee, and Bereiter-Engelmann. Children attended preschool for six and a half hours a day, five days a week, during one school year. Although some children from all programs entered Follow Through classes rather than regular kindergarten classes after completing preschool, post-preschool educational experience was not systematically varied by the experimenters as in the Karnes study. Approximately 200 children participated in the four programs.

## Di Lorenzo comparison of prekindergarten programs

In 1965, Louis T. Di Lorenzo undertook a longitudinal study of preschool programs implemented by eight school districts in New York State (Di Lorenzo, Salter, & Brady, 1969). Program types were not systematically varied by the experimenter but selected and/or developed and implemented by each school district. Program operation within each district was documented, and programs were differentiated along two continua: degree of structure and degree of cognitive-language orientation. Children attended half-day preschool programs during one school year. In seven of the districts, preschool classes were held five days per week. In the eighth, classes were held four days per week, the fifth day being devoted to parent-teacher conferences and home visits by teachers. Following the completion of preschool, children entered regular kindergarten classes. Approximately 1800 children participated in the study.

## Planned Variation Head Start

Planned Variation Head Start was initiated by the U.S. Office of Economic Opportunity in 1968 and administered by the U.S. Office of Child Development. It became operational in the fall of 1969. Program descriptions and research findings are presented in numerous reports (e.g., Bissell, 1971 and 1972; Stanford Research Institute, 1971; McDaniels et al., 1972; Walker, Bane, & Bryk, 1973; Lukas & Wohleb, 1972; Featherstone, 1973; Beller, 1973; Smith, 1973). Eight preschool programs were compared during the three years of the project. Four additional programs were included in Year 2; three additional programs, in Year 3. The Stanford Research Institute report (1971) classified programs into three categories: *pre-academic* models, emphasizing the development of specific pre-academic skills through drill, individualized programmed instruction, and systematic reinforcement; *cognitive discovery* models, emphasizing the development of basic cognitive processes and concepts through active exploration and verbal interaction; and *discovery* models, emphasizing the development of the "whole child" through free exploration and self-expression. The Cognitively Oriented Curriculum, one of the three programs of the CD Project, was selected as one of the eight Planned Variation curricula. In all programs, children attended preschool for one school year (four-year-old year, or five-year-old year if no kindergarten was available). The length of time spent in preschool classes each week varied substantially across sites. Following preschool, children entered either kindergarten or first grade in regular or Follow Through classes. About 1500 children participated in the project during Year 1; this number approximately doubled during the second and third years.

## CD Project design in relation to that of other preschool comparison studies

In order to interpret the findings of particular studies and to compare findings across studies, it is necessary to examine their experimental designs. What is being compared within a single study? Are the same programs compared in two different studies? Are the bases of program comparison (measures) comparable within and across studies?

### Program comparisons within a single study

With respect to the projects considered here, it is essential to know what is being compared in order to interpret findings of difference or similarity in program effects, i.e., to determine what explains the observed effects.

Any preschool program has many components which may influence child outcomes, and any or all of these components may differentiate one program from another. Among these are the following:

- characteristics of teachers
- characteristics of children
- curriculum model

- actual classroom process
- staff/child ratio and level of adult-child interaction (particularly purposive interaction)
- length of preschool day, week, year, and full program
- nature of parent involvement, if any
- methods of supervision or quality control
- teacher involvement in systematic day-to-day planning and evaluation
- physical aspects of the preschool classroom unrelated to curriculum model
- general structure and method of program administration

The unique, joint, and interactive effects of these and other components on child outcomes are only beginning to be explored. What is being compared is determined by the way in which (and the extent to which) an experimental design systematically varies and controls these basic components across programs and also by the pattern of effects across programs of components that are not controlled in the experimental design.

Although the unique effect of a program component can be isolated by varying it across programs while holding other components constant, in actual practice it is far more likely that the effects of several components will be confounded across programs. In such situations, no simple explanation of the observed outcomes is possible. For example, if two programs which have different curriculum models, classroom processes, teacher characteristics, physical facilities, and levels of parent involvement produce different outcomes in two comparable groups of children, who is to say which independent variables made a difference?

The preschool programs compared in the Karnes, Miller and Dyer, Di Lorenzo, and Planned Variation Head Start studies varied with respect to so many components that it is difficult to explain findings of difference or similarity except in global terms, i.e., that they were due to overall program differences or similarities. A further consideration when examining the effects of program components is the distinction between curriculum and noncurriculum variables. Although findings of differences in classroom processes are usually explained in terms of differences in curriculum models, noncurriculum components (e.g., length of program, staff/child ratio) can also exert considerable influence on what occurs in the classroom.

In the Karnes study, preschool programs varied not only in curriculum models but in child characteristics (middle-class children were included in community-integrated classrooms), levels of teacher training, staff/child ratios, supervision, post-preschool experience (children from two programs entered special kindergarten programs), and so forth. Moreover, the Montessori program was forced to abandon a fundamental component of its curriculum model by excluding younger (three-year-old) and older (five-year-old) children from the classroom.

In the Miller and Dyer study, programs varied in their administration-supervision, degree of teacher training and curriculum implementation, and presence or absence of home teaching activities. As in the Karnes study, the Montessori model was altered by including only four-year-olds in the class.

In the Di Lorenzo study, preschool programs were not systematically varied by the experimenter, and programs differed in length of educational treatment, staff/child ratios, administration-supervision, child characteristics, teacher training, parent involvement, noncurriculum physical aspects of classrooms, degree of model articulation and implementation, community environments, and so forth.

In Planned Variation Head Start, not only did preschool programs implemented by various sponsors differ in many of their components, but programs implemented by the same sponsor at different sites also tended to vary substantially from one another, perhaps reflecting local operational issues.

In the CD Project, an attempt was made to systematically vary curriculum models and associated classroom processes while holding other components as constant as possible across the three programs. This design was explicitly intended to address the question whether curriculum-specific variables in preschool programs, rather than other program components, are associated with particular child outcomes. The degree to which the experimental design of the CD Project succeeded in isolating curriculum variables from other sources of program variance will be examined further in succeeding chapters.

None of this discussion is intended to suggest that one of these preschool studies has a more valuable contribution to make than the others. Rather it urges careful consideration and interpretation of all findings, acknowledging the limitations which the experimental designs and operational constraints of various studies place upon inferences made.

## Comparisons within and across studies

The problems which arise in comparing and integrating findings from two or more studies are closely related to the problems encountered when interpreting findings of difference or similarity in program effects within a single study. No two preschool comparison studies to date have had the same experimental designs. Because such studies have compared various preschool programs in differing social-cultural contexts, using different measures obtained at different intervals, and have analyzed data using different statistical procedures, apparent differences and similarities in research findings should be interpreted very cautiously.

When the findings of different studies seem to confirm one another, one is inclined either to overlook differences in experimental designs (treating one study as a replication of the other) or to conclude that similar findings obtained under somewhat different experimental conditions offer even stronger confirmation than mere replication. When the findings from different studies contradict each other, one examines the experimental design of each study in an attempt to ferret out some reasonable explanation of the contradiction. In either case, conclusions are at best "educated guesses." The difficulties involved in integrating findings from the CD Project with those from other preschool comparison studies are discussed in chapter VI.

The contents of the remaining chapters of this report are as follows:

**Chapter II** provides a description of the CD Project's research design, characteristics of sample children, and the noncurriculum variables which were held constant across the three programs.

**Chapter III** documents the operation of the three preschool programs in classrooms and in children's homes. Findings from three observation procedures are presented—systematic classroom observations, observations by national consultants, and home visit observations by teachers.

**Chapters IV and V** present information on child outcomes through grade 4. Chapter IV reports on ratings by teachers and parents of project children as they progress from preschool through grade 4. Chapter V presents the results of children's testing at different timepoints on various cognitive and linguistic measures.

**Chapter VI** contains a summary and discussion of the major research findings of the CD Project.

# II Research design

As noted in the preceding chapter, the central purpose of the CD Project was to compare the effects of different preschool curricula on the concurrent and longitudinal development of economically disadvantaged children at high academic risk. Three contrasting curricula were implemented: *Cognitive*—the High/Scope Foundation's Cognitively Oriented Curriculum (Weikart et al., 1971); *Language*—Bereiter and Engelmann's Language Training Curriculum (Bereiter & Engelmann, 1966); and *Unit-Based*—a curriculum representing the American nursery school tradition (McClelland et al., 1970). Since the CD Project was designed to address the question whether curriculum-specific variables in preschool programs, rather than other program components, are associated with particular child outcomes, noncurriculum variables were held constant across the three programs. In this chapter, the characteristics of the sample children are described, followed by a description of the noncurriculum operational variables or setting variables, which were held constant.

# THE SAMPLE

The CD Project sample was drawn from families living in Ypsilanti, Michigan, population 30,000 (combined city and township population: 63,000). Ypsilanti, contiguous with Ann Arbor, is located 30 miles west of Detroit in southern Michigan's transportation and industrial corridor. Ypsilanti is a microcosm of large midwestern cities. The economic base of the city is diverse and its population heterogeneous. Although the 18,000 students who attend Eastern Michigan University are a major element in the life of the community, the resident population is predominantly working-class. In fact, the city and township employ some 23,000 people in over 60 industries (primarily automotive, plastics, modular home manufacturing, and paper manufacturing). Housing ranges from densely populated tenements and projects to sprawling suburban homes. Black families comprise 25% of the total population and reside predominantly on the southern side of town. Many heads of both black and white households are immigrants from southern states.

Four criteria defined the sample universe of the CD Project. Eligible families (1) lived within Ypsilanti public school attendance areas, (2) were of low socio-economic status (SES), and (3) had three-year-old children who (4) scored substantially below average on the Stanford-Binet Intelligence Scale. The Stanford-Binet and SES selection criteria were used to identify children in the community at the highest levels of academic risk, i.e., children most likely to fail in school.

## SES criterion

Socio-economic status was determined through parent interviews using an SES rating scale (the Family Preschool Data Scale) which is described later in this chapter. The scale, originally developed for the Ypsilanti Perry Preschool Project, included the following components:

- *Occupation* of father (or of mother if no father was living in the home) on a five-point scale:
  1 = unemployed
  2 = unskilled
  3 = semiskilled
  4 = skilled
  5 = professional
- *Education* (years) completed by parents (an average of the two, or the mother's education if no father was living in the home)
- *Density* in the home, defined as the number of rooms (kitchen and bathroom included, shared bath counted as one-half) divided by the number of people living in the home

Each component was weighted. First, the scores on each component were converted to standard scores; that is, each score was divided by the approximate standard deviation for that component (2 for Education, ½ for Occupation, ¼ for Density). Density was given one-half the weight of the other two variables. The summation of these variables produced the SES rating. The computational formula was:

$$\text{SES} = \frac{\text{Education}}{s_{\text{ed}}} + \frac{\text{Occupation}}{s_{\text{occ}}} + \frac{1}{2}\left\langle \frac{\text{Density}}{s_{\text{den}}} \right\rangle$$

where s is the standard deviation for the component.

In the preliminary (1967-68) survey of families with preschool-age children living in the Ypsilanti School District, SES ratings ranged from 5.3 to 16.8. Following a careful review of SES and other demographic data, it was decided that only families with SES ratings of 11 or below would be eligible for the project. In the judgment of CD Project staff, Ypsilanti families within that SES range were comparable to poor, inner-city families in most northern industrial cities.

## Stanford-Binet criterion

Children of families who met the SES criterion were administered the Stanford-Binet Intelligence Scale, Form L-M (Terman & Merrill, 1960). Deviation IQs (1960 norms) on the Binet are reported and analyzed in this report.

State of Michigan special education guidelines defining "educable mental retardation" were used to establish the eligibility cutoff points in Binet scores. Applying the guidelines which existed at that time, children scoring at least one standard deviation below (but not more than three standard deviations below) the population mean and with no evidence of organic impairment were eligible for enrollment in the CD Project. Some children with Binet IQ scores higher than 84 were enrolled because of the difficulty of finding enough children within the educable mentally retarded range. Pretreatment Binet scores in the longitudinal sample ranged from 62 through 90.

# Sampling

During September of each project year (1967-1969), Ypsilanti Public School District census data were used to locate all families that had three-year-old children. These families were then interviewed to obtain information for computing SES ratings. Next, children of families with SES ratings at or below 11 were tested with the Binet. Children who met the Binet criterion as described above became eligible for project enroll- ment. Virtually all eligible children were enrolled in the project during its three years of operation. In other words, the sample coincided with the eligible population, excluding a few children who were already enrolled in other preschool or day-care programs.

# Waves[7]

Four waves of children participated in the CD Project from 1967 through 1970. The CD Project followed the Ypsilanti Perry Preschool Project (1962-1967), which was run in five waves, numbered from 0 through 4. Hence the four waves of the CD Project were numbered 5 through 8. Waves 5 through 8 are described as follows:

**Wave 5 (n = 27).** Wave 5 was transitional from the Perry Project to the CD Project. Children in Wave 5 entered the CD Project as four-year-olds in 1967 and were "senior preschoolers" to children in Wave 6. As three- year-olds, children in Wave 5 had had differing educational experiences:

- Children entering the Cognitive Program had been in the experimen- tal group of the Perry Project (Weikart et al., 1978).
- Children entering the Language Program had been in the control group of the Perry Project.
- Children entering the Unit-Based Program were newly selected in 1967.

Since children in Wave 5 experienced different educational programs as three-year-olds and were not enrolled for two consecutive years in one of the three CD Project programs, they are not included in the longitudinal sample.

**Wave 6 and Wave 7 (n = 41).** Children in Waves 6 and 7 were enrolled in the CD Project as three-year-olds in 1967 and 1968, respectively. Each child in Waves 6 and 7 attended two years of preschool in one of the three CD Project programs. Children from Wave 6 entered kindergarten in fall 1969; children from Wave 7 in fall 1970. These two waves constitute the sample of the longitudinal study reported here. (Although Waves 6 and 7 were originally intended to represent two replications of the experiment,

---

[7]A wave is defined as one group of subjects in a series of replications in which all major aspects of a study (i.e., sample characteristics, design, treatment, and measures) are held constant for each replication. A wave is a special instance of a cohort, a term which refers to the temporal sequencing of groups but does not imply that the essential research dimensions are held constant.

pretreatment differences among treatment groups within waves (discussed in the next section) and the small number of children in each wave (19 and 22) make it necessary to combine the two waves for purposes of data analysis.)

**Wave 8 (n = 24).**   Wave 8 children were enrolled in the CD Project in order to maintain a cross-age grouping in each program during the final year of the project. Children in Wave 8 were enrolled as three-year-olds in fall 1969 and were "junior preschoolers" to children in Wave 7 (who were in their second preschool year). After the CD Project terminated in spring 1970 with the graduation of Wave 7, all children in Wave 8 were enrolled in the Cognitive Program as four-year-olds. Since Wave 8 children did not receive the same treatment as children in Waves 6 and 7, they are not included in the longitudinal sample.

## Assignment of children to treatment groups

The assignment of children in Wave 5 to treatment conditions was described briefly in the preceding section. Children in Waves 6 through 8 were assigned to treatment groups according to the procedures described in this section.

Following each year's sample selection, children with siblings already in the project were assigned to the same program as their siblings. Nine children were assigned to treatment groups in this manner from 1967 through 1969. The remaining children in each wave were divided into three groups of equal size matched, as far as possible, according to ethnicity, sex, and age. Twins were always assigned to the same group. These groups were then randomly assigned to treatment conditions.

Chance differences in pretreatment Binet means among treatment groups in Wave 6 necessitated reassignment of several children in Wave 7 in order to achieve overall comparability in pretreatment Binet means among the three treatment groups. This was accomplished by exchanging children of the same sex, age, and ethnicity but different pretreatment Binet scores among the three groups. Although this procedure violated the initial random assignment within waves, decisions to reassign children were made solely on the basis of the criteria already described and introduced no apparent bias favoring one group over another.

## Characteristics of children in the three treatment groups

Since the statistical analyses and inferences made in the remainder of this report assume that children in the three treatment groups were samples from the same population, it is important to evaluate the effects which the departures from random assignment described above may have had upon treatment-group composition. As noted in an earlier section, information on group composition was obtained prior to enrollment through a structured parent interview, using the Family Preschool Data Scale (FPDS). Comparisons of pretreatment variables derived from the FPDS for children in the Cognitive, Language, and Unit-Based programs—Waves 6 and 7 combined—are given in tables 1 and 2.

Categorical variables are shown in table 1. No statistically significant[8] differences in distributions across groups (chi-square) were found on any measures: sex of child, ethnicity of child, presence of father in home, employment of mother, and employment of head of household. Likewise, no differences were found in comparisons of continuous variables across treatment groups (analysis of variance—table 2): child's age at enrollment, pretreatment Binet, number of children in family, number of older children, number of younger children, SES, parental education, household density, and parental occupational status. The absence of statistically significant group differences on pretreatment measures provides strong evidence that children in the Cognitive, Language, and Unit-Based programs represent independent samples drawn from the same population, and this assumption will be made in the remainder of the report.

**Table 1**

*Chi-Square Tests of the Distribution of
Pretreatment Characteristics Across Treatment Groups
(Waves 6 and 7)*

| Variables | Cognitive Group (N = 11) | | Language Group (N = 15) | | Unit-Based Group (N = 15) | | $X^2$ |
|---|---|---|---|---|---|---|---|
| | N | % | N | % | N | % | |
| Male | 5 | 46 | 8 | 53 | 9 | 60 | 0.54 |
| Female | 6 | 54 | 7 | 47 | 6 | 40 | n.s. |
| Black | 6 | 54 | 7 | 47 | 8 | 53 | 0.20 |
| White | 5 | 46 | 8 | 53 | 7 | 47 | n.s. |
| Father Present in Home | 8 | 73 | 11 | 73 | 13 | 87 | 1.03 |
| Father Absent | 3 | 27 | 4 | 27 | 2 | 13 | n.s. |
| Mother Employed | 3 | 27 | 7 | 47 | 4 | 27 | 1.65 |
| Mother Unemployed | 8 | 73 | 8 | 53 | 11 | 73 | n.s. |
| Head of Household: | | | | | | | |
| Unemployed (on welfare) | 2 | 18 | 2 | 13 | 2 | 13 | 0.54 |
| Employed (unskilled) | 8 | 73 | 12 | 80 | 11 | 73 | n.s. |
| Employed (semi-skilled) | 1 | 9 | 1 | 7 | 2 | 13 | |

## Sample attrition

Fewer than 10% of children enrolled in the CD Project dropped out before completing two years in preschool. All of these children moved out of the

---

[8] A probability level of .05 is considered significant throughout this report unless otherwise indicated.

**Table 2**

*One-Way Analyses of Variance by Treatment Group*
*of Pretreatment Characteristics*

| Variable | Cognitive Group (N=11) | | Language Group (N=15) | | Unit-Based Group (N=15) | | F Ratio |
|---|---|---|---|---|---|---|---|
| | Mean | S D | Mean | S D | Mean | S D | |
| SES Rating | 9.3 | 1.00 | 8.9 | 0.81 | 9.1 | 1.02 | < 1 |
| Socio-Economic Index[a] | 18.3 | 11.93 | 16.4 | 7.97 | 19.7 | 12.10 | < 1 |
| Pretreatment Binet IQ | 80.5 | 6.77 | 81.9 | 5.82 | 79.7 | 7.49 | < 1 |
| Child's Age at Entry (in months) | 40.8 | 3.03 | 40.9 | 3.91 | 39.8 | 2.93 | < 1 |
| Parents' Average Education | 9.7 | 1.59 | 9.6 | 1.18 | 10.0 | 1.29 | < 1 |
| Father's Education | 9.7 | 1.87 | 9.0 | 1.63 | 8.8 | 2.68 | < 1 |
| Mother's Education | 9.5 | 2.81 | 10.1 | 1.53 | 11.1 | 0.74 | 2.78 |
| Head of Household's Employment Level[b] | 1.9 | 0.54 | 1.9 | 0.46 | 2.0 | 0.53 | < 1 |
| Father's Employment Level[b] | 2.1 | 0.33 | 2.1 | 0.30 | 2.2 | 0.38 | < 1 |
| Mother's Employment Level[b] | 1.2 | 0.40 | 1.5 | 0.52 | 1.3 | 0.46 | 1.32 |
| Density in Home (persons/room) | 1.0 | 0.39 | 1.1 | 0.42 | 1.2 | 0.46 | 1.28 |
| Number of People in Household | 5.5 | 1.97 | 5.9 | 2.17 | 6.7 | 3.29 | < 1 |
| Number of Rooms in Home | 5.7 | 1.62 | 5.7 | 1.18 | 5.5 | 2.10 | < 1 |
| Number of Children in Family | 3.5 | 2.42 | 3.5 | 2.39 | 3.6 | 2.50 | < 1 |
| Number of Older Siblings | 2.2 | 2.36 | 1.7 | 2.22 | 2.1 | 2.02 | < 1 |
| Number of Younger Siblings | 0.3 | 0.47 | 0.8 | 0.94 | 0.5 | 0.83 | 1.39 |

[a]Duncan Socio-Economic Index (Robinson, Athanasiou, & Head, 1969) with the additional assignment of 01 as a score to those unemployed.

[b]Code for employment levels: 0 = no data
    1 = unemployed
    2 = unskilled employment
    3 = semi-skilled employment
    4 = skilled employment (including lower managerial)
    5 = professional employment (no cases in sample)

Ypsilanti Public School District with their families. Two children were excluded from the sample after completing two years of preschool because a routine verification of their original SES ratings revealed that they were not, in fact, eligible.

Sample attrition during the longitudinal phase of the study has been slight. In fourth grade, only 3 of the 41 children in the project were not contacted.

# DESCRIPTION OF NONCURRICULUM VARIABLES

## Structure of the programs

Each of the three programs in the CD Project had two major components: half-day preschool sessions for the child and home visits with mother and child. Home visits, lasting 90 minutes, were made every two weeks by one of the child's classroom teachers. The purpose of the home visits was to involve mothers in helping their children learn at home. Teachers encouraged mothers to "teach" their children in the same manner as they were being "taught" in preschool. "Teaching," of course, meant something quite different in each program, as indicated by the curriculum descriptions in chapter I.

## Setting of the programs

The three preschool programs were housed in two one-room country schools located within two miles of each other in Ypsilanti township. For the first six months of the CD Project, the Cognitive and Language programs shared one of the schoolrooms; one program operated in the morning and the other in the afternoon. The Unit-Based Program was housed in the other school, which also provided office space for project administrative staff. The Language Program, however, did not require the same materials and equipment that were used in both the Cognitive and Unit-Based programs. Therefore it seemed advisable for the Language and Unit-Based programs to switch places, and this was done in summer 1968.

## The teachers

Each of the three preschool programs in the CD Project had its own teaching team each year. Table 3 shows the assignment of teachers to programs over the three-year project. The composition of the Language Program team changed at the end of each project year, and that of the Cognitive team changed during the second year. The Unit-Based team remained constant across all three project years. One teaching aide (resident of the school district) was also assigned to each program. The aides assumed teaching roles in the classroom under the direction of regular

**Table 3**

*Teacher Assignments in the CD Project*

| Project Year | Program | | | | | |
|---|---|---|---|---|---|---|
| | Cognitive (4 teachers) | | Language (5 teachers) | | Unit-Based (2 teachers) | |
| I<br>1967-1968<br>(Waves 5 & 6) | Teacher A[1] | Teacher B | Teacher E | Teacher F | Teacher J | Teacher K |
| II<br>1968-1969<br>(Waves 6 & 7) | Teacher C | Teacher D | Teacher G | Teacher H | | |
| III<br>1969-1970<br>(Waves 7 & 8) | | | Teacher I | | | |

[1]Letter suffixes correspond to those of Weikart (1972) where individual teachers and their experiences are described in detail.

classroom teachers. Aides remained the same for the duration of the CD Project.

In addition to teachers and aides, a "helper" was assigned to each program. Helpers were high-school girls recruited from special-education classes in Ypsilanti, Michigan who were paid and also received school credit for their work in the preschool. Although the roles of helpers varied somewhat from day to day and year to year (as helpers changed), in the main they provided custodial care for the children (e.g., when riding the bus to and from school or on field trips) and helped maintain the classrooms.

Other teacher-related, noncurriculum variables that were held constant across the three programs are listed below:

- Teaching teams in all three programs engaged in daily evaluation and planning sessions for both individual children and groups. Aides were included in these evaluation/planning sessions. Teachers and aides in each program met separately from those in the other programs to ensure that theories and practices employed in the three curricula did not influence one another.

- All three teaching teams were closely supervised. One staff member assumed major responsibility for supervision of the three teams. Supervision focused primarily on facilitating and sustaining day-to-day team evaluation and planning in order to keep teachers closely in touch with both curriculum goals and the needs of individual children.

- Each program was frequently reviewed by nonteaching staff and by outside consultants who observed in the classroom and met with teachers and the supervisor. The review process helped to ensure faithful implementation of curriculum models.

- In each program, teachers made home visits during the half-day that preschool classes were not in session. Teachers filled out Home Visit

Reports to help them evaluate the progress of individual children and discussed these reports with the supervisor.

- An attempt was made to assign equally qualified teachers to each program.
- All three curricula were administered as part of the same research project with identical funding, personnel policies, and infrastructure.

## Other noncurriculum variables

Other noncurriculum variables were held constant across the three programs to reduce the confounding of curriculum-specific with curriculum-irrelevant variables:

- All children attended preschool for 2½ hours a day, five days a week, during the school year.
- The staff/child ratio (excluding helpers) was maintained at 1 to 5 for each program.
- The children in each program rode separate buses to and from school each day.

## SUMMARY

Although the central research question in this study is simply stated:

*Do different preschool curricula, faithfully implemented, have different effects on children?*

its answer is complex. Comparisons of outcomes for children in the Cognitive, Language, and Unit-Based programs will reveal program-related effects only if the research design has controlled other variables which might account for differential outcomes in the three groups. In preceding sections of this chapter, efforts to hold curriculum-irrelevant operational variables constant across the three programs have been described, and the assumption that children in the three treatment groups were comparable at enrollment (i.e., were samples from the same population) has been defended. However, one important noncurriculum variable—teachers—did vary across programs.

Children in each program not only experienced different curricula but different teachers as well. That is to say, teacher effects were completely confounded with curriculum effects in the experimental design. Had a large number of teachers implemented each curriculum (and ideally been randomly assigned to programs), it might be possible to conclude that teachers were "comparable" across programs. However, this was clearly not the case in the CD Project. It might seem, then, that the curriculum comparison study is thereby reduced to a teacher comparison study.

Evidence that the CD Project did more than compare teachers is presented in chapter III, which examines educational processes in the three preschool programs. To the extent that the educational process systematically differed in ways predicted by or compatible with curriculum models, it can be argued that comparisons of outcomes across treatment groups reveal curriculum or program effects rather than idiosyncratic teacher effects. Data reported in chapter III provide strong evidence that implementation in the programs was faithful to three distinct curriculum models and that educational processes differed in expected ways. Consequently, comparisons of outcomes across treatments reveal effects which are largely curriculum- or program-related.

# III Operation of the programs

This chapter documents the operation of the Cognitive, Language, and Unit-Based preschool programs in classrooms and in children's homes. The findings of three different observational procedures are presented:

- Systematic observation of classroom behavior
- Observation of classroom behavior by consultants
- Reports of home visits by teachers

# SYSTEMATIC OBSERVATION OF CLASSROOM BEHAVIOR

Systematic observation of classroom behavior has recently assumed a central role in educational research and evaluation; when the CD Project began, however, it was a relatively novel method. Three trial systems of observation used in the CD Project are reported here for their methodological value. These first attempts paved the way for an approach to systematic observation that meets present standards of reliability and validity— the Pupil Record of School Experience (PROSE), developed by Medley, Schluck and Ames (1968b).

In this section, findings from the PROSE are reported in detail, following the descriptions of the three preliminary attempts at systematic observation. In addition, PROSE findings are related to the major curriculum expectations of each CD Project program. The PROSE provides dramatic evidence that the three programs operated differently from one another and in accordance with the curriculum models they were selected to represent.

## First attempts

The Observation Schedule and Record (OScAR), the Cognitive and Language Observation Scales (CLOS), and the Behavior Observation Rating Scale (BORS) were the three observation systems used in the CD Project before the PROSE was adopted. The OScAR, Version 5, was developed by Medley, Schluck and Ames (1968a) to categorize the speech of teachers and children in teacher-led groups. It was used in the first project year (Seifert, 1969) and again in the second project year (Seifert, 1970a). The CLOS was developed by Seifert (1970b) to categorize teacher behavior specific to the Cognitive and Language curricula. The BORS was developed by Sheriff (1970) in an attempt to complement the other two systems by focusing on social interaction among children in the absence of the teacher. Both the CLOS and the BORS were used during the second project year.

As first attempts, the OScAR, CLOS, and BORS demonstrated that systematic observation was useful in documenting program processes and comparing program effects in the CD Project. Two problems, however, plagued these three observational systems: a lack of sufficient inter-observer reliability and a lack of generalizability from observations to programs. The latter problem arose because the observations were too brief and the activities observed were not comparable across programs. However, it should be added that the evolution of these instruments was and continues to be instructive to those who would use observational systems. The OScAR and the CLOS could be useful in teacher-centered programs. Child-centered programs are frequent among preschools and are more sensitively observed with child-centered instruments, such as the PROSE, which is described in the following pages.[9]

## The PROSE[10]

The Pupil Record of School Experience, or PROSE, was developed by Medley, Schluck and Ames (1968b) to describe classroom behavior as it relates to individual children, particularly preschool children (Medley, 1969). This observation system solved the problem of generalizability from observations to different program settings and to different types of interactions since all such settings and interactions could be observed. Also, as described below, inter-observer reliability was demonstrated in most categories of the PROSE.

### PROSE categories

Figure 2 lists, in decision-tree format, the PROSE categories used and analyzed in the CD Project. The focus of the observation was on the individual child: the child's activity level (low and moderate), the nature of the activity (fantasy, work, purposeful, nonpurposeful), and the setting of the activity (a social interaction with an adult[11] or another child or an interaction with materials). If the child was alone and interacting with materials the only other category coded concerned how the child was attending to the task. If, however, the child was engaged in a social inter-action, several additional categories were coded.

To determine the role of "peer(s) toward child," the observer simply coded the peer behavior (initiating, attending, refusing). To determine the role of "child toward adults," the first question considered was whether or not an adult was attending to the child. If not, the child's relationship to the adult was coded as either active initiation or passive attention. If, on the other hand, the adult *was* attending to the child, the interaction was coded as the child either receiving the adult's attention or as being in a group to which the adult was attending. If the adult was expressing strong, nonroutine feelings and was not involved in procedural matters,

---

[9]These efforts have been extended and several new instruments have been developed by High/Scope Foundation staff which are even more sensitive to classroom processes in programs emphasizing child-initiated learning. New instruments include the Child Observation Record (COR), Classroom Implementation Checklist (CIC), Analysis of Classroom Interaction (ACI), Systematic Classroom Observation of Pupil Experience (SCOPE), and Systematic Classroom Observation of Teacher Experience (SCOTE).

[10]The use of the PROSE in the CD Project was previously reported in Sheriff, 1971.

[11]The adult involved in these interactions was either an aide or a teacher. The aides were either adults or teenagers. All of the adults in the CD Project were women.

**Figure 2**

*PROSE Categories in Decision-Tree Format*

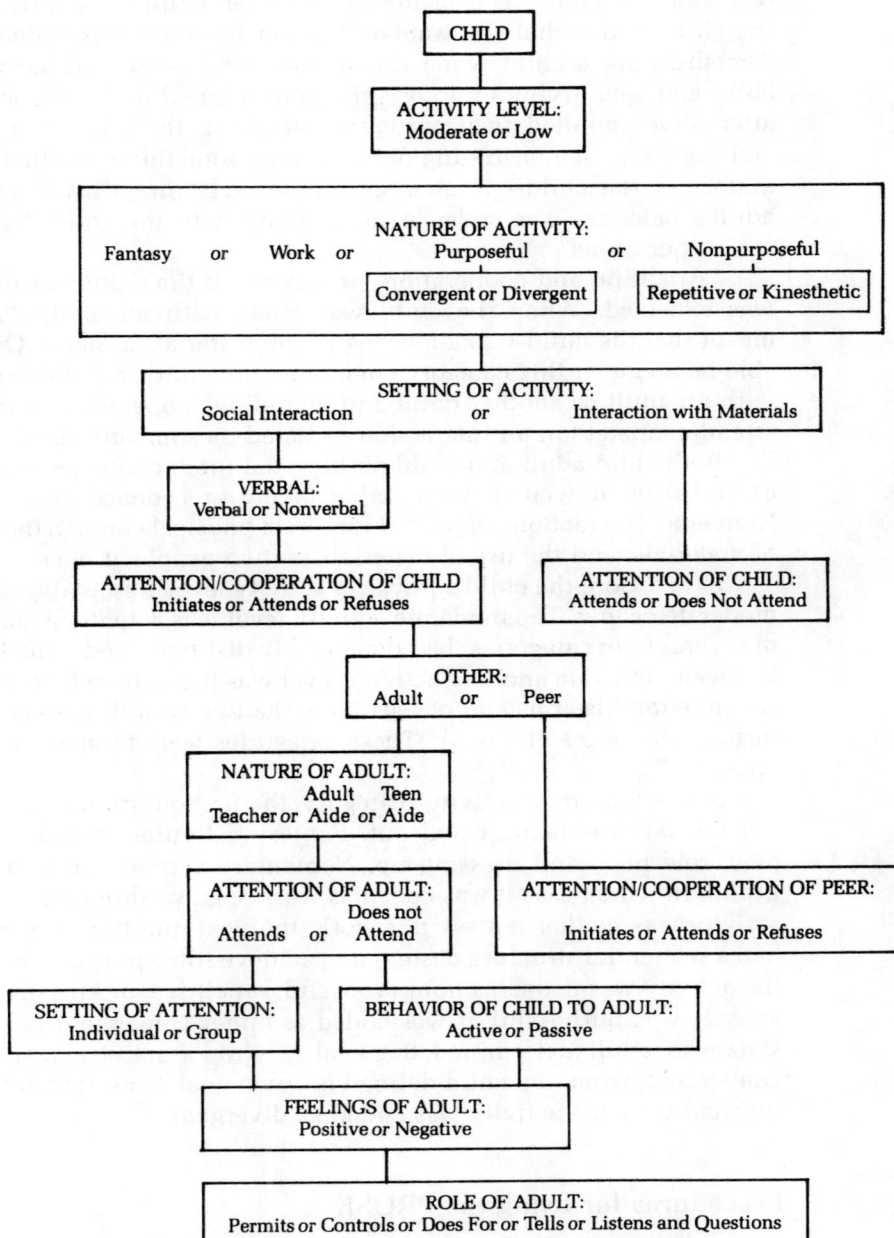

```
                        ┌─────────────┐
                        │    CHILD    │
                        └─────────────┘
                        ┌─────────────────────┐
                        │ ACTIVITY LEVEL:     │
                        │ Moderate or Low     │
                        └─────────────────────┘
```

NATURE OF ACTIVITY:
Fantasy   or   Work   or   Purposeful   or   Nonpurposeful
                           Convergent or Divergent     Repetitive or Kinesthetic

SETTING OF ACTIVITY:
Social Interaction        or        Interaction with Materials

VERBAL:
Verbal or Nonverbal

ATTENTION/COOPERATION OF CHILD
Initiates or Attends or Refuses

ATTENTION OF CHILD:
Attends or Does Not Attend

OTHER:
Adult   or   Peer

NATURE OF ADULT:
Adult      Teen
Teacher or Aide or Aide

ATTENTION OF ADULT:
Does not
Attends   or   Attend

ATTENTION/COOPERATION OF PEER:
Initiates or Attends or Refuses

SETTING OF ATTENTION:
Individual or Group

BEHAVIOR OF CHILD TO ADULT:
Active or Passive

FEELINGS OF ADULT:
Positive or Negative

ROLE OF ADULT:
Permits or Controls or Does For or Tells or Listens and Questions

NOTE: When the behavior involves more than one category on the same horizontal line, the category on the far left takes precedence.

her behavior was coded as either positive or negative. (It should be noted that the routine positive reinforcement in the Language Program did not fall into this category.) Also in this category, the adult's behavior was coded as giving permission when either encouraging a child to make a choice or allowing the child to engage in a chosen activity. The adult's behavior was coded as exerting control over a child if she was pressing the child to do what she wanted, but her behavior was coded as doing something for a child when this action involved something which the child had been trying to do or apparently wished to do. If none of these alternatives applied to a particular situation, the adult was coded as "telling," i.e., demonstrating or explaining something, reading or telling a story to the child—what might be termed "direct teaching." Or the adult's behavior was coded as conversing with the child, listening, or asking questions.

"Attention and cooperation" was coded if the child was doing what was expected. When the child was alone with materials, "attention" meant that the child was attending to the materials at hand. Other code-able behavior in this category concerned the child initiating interaction with an adult or another child and attending/cooperating or refusing to attend/cooperate in an interaction initiated by someone else.

Both child-adult and child-child social interactions were also coded as verbal or nonverbal, with verbal taking precedence over nonverbal. Nonverbal interaction was coded for direct physical contact, the exchange of materials, and the use of materials by two people at once.

In addition, the child's physical activity level was analyzed as either moderate or low. The moderate activity level was actually a combination of several finer categories, less dependably distinguished. The distinction between moderate and low activity level was based on whether the child was moving his arms and/or legs more than he would in an activity like turning the pages of a book. These categories were termed "active" and "passive."

In the "nature of activity" category, the first question was whether or not fantasy was being acted out. Fantasy activities included dramatic play, role play, and dressing up. Nonfantasy activity could be socially useful, in which case it was coded as work, e.g., washing off a table. If an activity was neither fantasy nor work, the next question was whether it had a sequential structure designed to achieve some purpose. If it did not, the activity was coded as nonpurposeful, repetitive, or kinesthetic; if the activity was purposeful, it was coded as either convergent or divergent. When an adult determined the goal, a child's activity was coded as convergent; when the child defined his own goal or used materials in an unusual way, the activity was coded as divergent.

## Procedures for using the PROSE

The PROSE was used in observation as follows. An observation was recorded at a point in time signaled every 25 seconds. A cycle of five such observations was recorded for one of four children, then for the second child, the third, and the fourth. The pattern was repeated with these four children for a total of three times. Then a second set of four children was observed, and so on, until all the children in the room were observed. This procedure continued throughout a program session. Each of the three programs was observed during ten sessions by at least one observer (two observers viewed four sessions so that inter-observer agreement could be assessed).

The Cognitive Program was observed during its afternoon session every other day that it met. The Language and Unit-Based programs were observed during their morning sessions on the days when the Cognitive Program was not observed. This schedule was followed five days a week for four weeks in the spring of the third project year (1970).

## PROSE inter-observer reliability

Table 4 presents percentages of inter-observer agreement for each PROSE category. The figures reported are percentages of agreement between two observers as computed by Cartwright's alpha (1956)—the number of agreements divided by the sum of agreements plus disagreements, determined on an event-by-event basis. The two observers viewed four program sessions together (including at least one session per program). The sessions were spread from the beginning to the end of the four weeks of observation. The inter-observer reliability for three-fifths of the PROSE categories was substantial (70% or greater). In many cases, a low percentage of agreement is attributable to low frequency of occurrence of a category. Percentages of agreement were taken into account in making program comparisons by the methods described in appendix A. Overall, the inter-observer reliability for this complex and lengthy set of categories was remarkably good.

## PROSE findings by category, across programs

Findings of systematic observation with the PROSE, across programs, are graphically represented in figures 3 through 11, and are summarized in table 5. The visual display of proportions in the figures provides clear evidence of program differences in a large number of categories. Table 5 indicates the results of statistical tests for program differences, measured against sampling error and observer error. The specific techniques are described in appendix A. A table of the raw frequencies of observed events in each category also appears in appendix A. The following discussion emphasizes program differences which were significant by these standards.

Figure 3 shows the three major types of interaction categories that organized most of the remaining PROSE categories: child-adult, child-child, and child-material. In each of the three preschool programs, the child was alone with materials about half the time; program differences were apparent, however, in both child-child and child-adult interactions. In all three programs, there was less social interaction between children than between children and adults. But this pattern was extreme in the Language Program where children interacted with adults nine times as often as with other children. In fact as well as in theory, interaction among

**Table 4**

*PROSE Categories and Percentage of Observer Agreement*

| | Percentage of Agreement | | |
| | Child Interacts With: | | |
| Category | Adult | Material | Child |
|---|---|---|---|
| **Role of Child Toward Adults:** | | | |
| Initiates interaction with adult | 88 | | |
| Receives individual attention from adult | 87 | | |
| In a group receiving adult attention | 89 | | |
| Gives attention to non-attending adult | 80 | | |
| **Adult Involved in Interaction:** | | | |
| Teacher | 98 | | |
| Adult Aide | 83 | | |
| Teenage Aide | 85 | | |
| **Adult Behavior:** | | | |
| Listens, questions; converses | 41 | | |
| Does something for child | 78 | | |
| Gives permission | 36 | | |
| Non-routine positive feeling | 40 | | |
| Non-routine negative feeling | (a) | | |
| Exerts control over child | 89 | | |
| Tells, explains; direct teaching | 86 | | |
| **Child Toward Other:** | | | |
| Child initiates interaction with peer | | | 61 |
| Child attends or cooperates | 95 | 93 | 76 |
| Child does not attend or cooperate | 45 | 79 | 83 |
| **Peer Toward Child:** | | | |
| Peer initiates interaction with child | | | 44 |
| Peer cooperates with child | | | 89 |
| Peer does not cooperate with child | | | 67 |
| **Mode of Interaction:** | | | |
| Verbal | 95 | | 70 |
| Nonverbal | 51 | | 64 |
| **Child's Activity Level:** | | | |
| Low | 67 | 57 | (a) |
| Moderate | 81 | 82 | 67 |
| **Nature of Activity (Across Types of Interaction):** | | | |
| Fantasy, role play | 77 | | |
| Divergent purpose, set by child | 62 | | |
| Convergent purpose, set by adult | 82 | | |
| Work, socially useful activity | 89 | | |
| Nonpurposeful repetitive activity | 58 | | |

NOTE: Percentage of agreement between two observers (Cartwright, 1956) during four sessions.

[a]Observer agreement undetermined because the category was coded less than ten times.

children was peripheral to the Language Program since it was more teacher-centered than either of the others. In both the Cognitive and Unit-Based programs, about one-quarter of the social interaction that occurred was between children.

Figure 4 presents a breakdown of child-adult interaction by the various "roles of child toward adult." In this category an area of clear program

**Figure 3**

*Object of Child's Interaction*

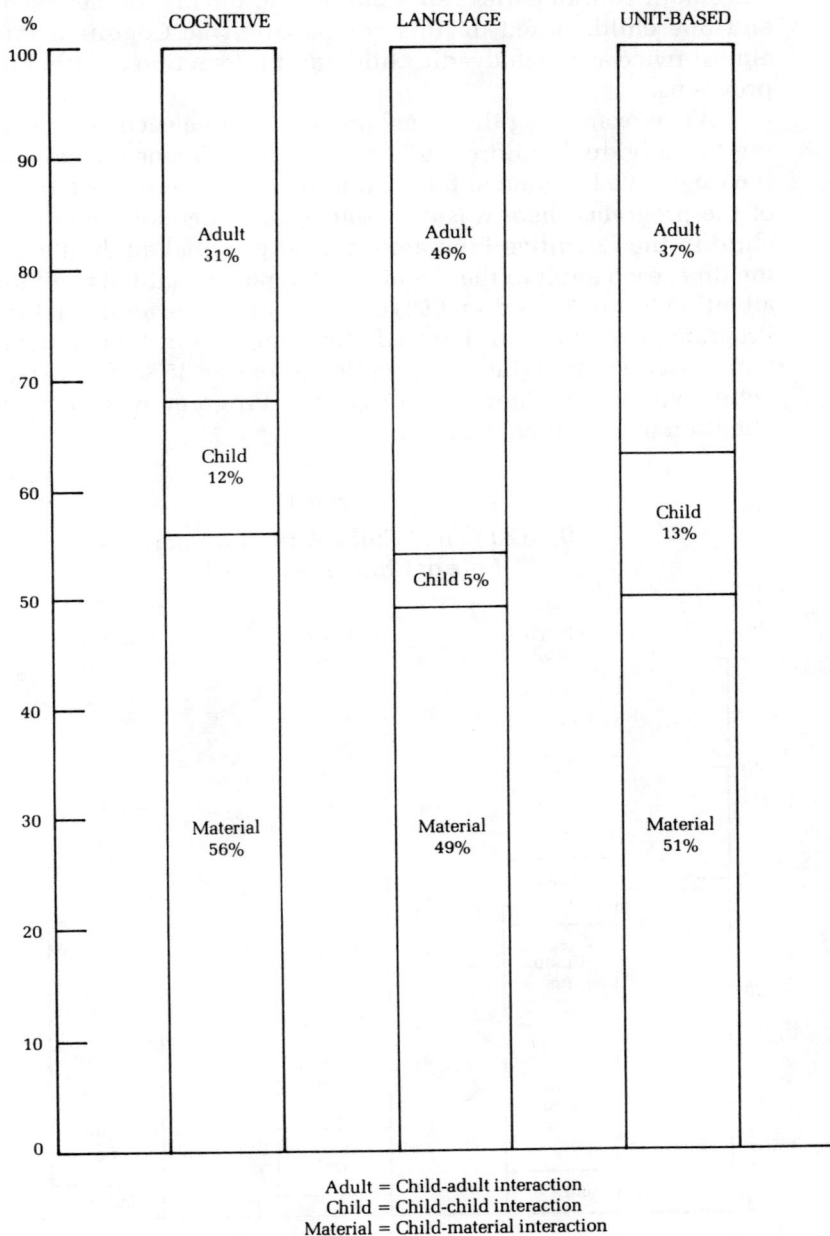

Adult = Child-adult interaction
Child = Child-child interaction
Material = Child-material interaction

distinction was "child receives individual attention" as opposed to "child in a group receiving attention." In the Language Program, children received five times as much adult attention in groups (29%) as when they were by themselves (6%), and in the Unit-Based Program they received almost three times as much attention in groups (19%) as when they were alone (7%). In contrast, a child in the Cognitive Program actually received more individual attention (13%) than group attention (9%).[12]

Further program distinctions can be found by combining "child receives individual attention" with "child initiates interaction with adult" since both subcategories represent dyadic interaction between one adult and one child. Based on this comparison, the Cognitive Program had almost twice as much dyadic child-adult interaction as either of the other programs.

When examining the actual amount of time each adult spent attending to individual children, a considerable difference is evident between the Cognitive Program and the other two. For every five children in each of the programs there was only one adult. Therefore, while the average child in the Cognitive Program received personal adult attention 13% of the time, each adult in the Cognitive Program actually was giving personal attention to 1 of 5 children 65% of the adult's time; adults in the Language Program gave children personal attention 30% of their time; and in the Unit-Based Program the comparable figure was 35%. From an adult interaction viewpoint, then, the Cognitive Program was characterized by attention to individual children.

**Figure 4**

*Breakdown of Child-Adult Interaction—*
*Role of Child Toward Adults*

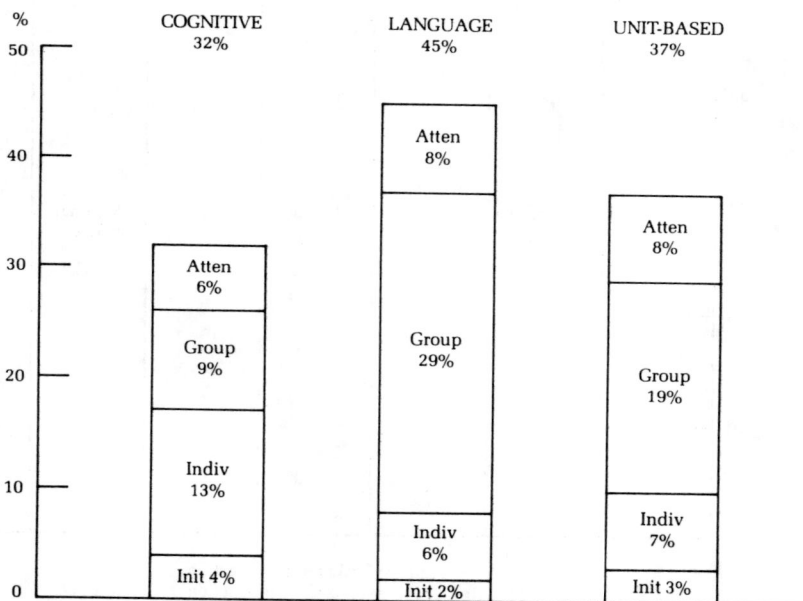

Atten = Child gives attention to adult who is
not attending to the child
Group = Child in a group receiving attention
Indiv = Child receives individual attention
Init = Child initiates interaction with adult

---

[12]Percentages in figures 4 through 10 may differ slightly from those in figure 3 due to rounding when total percentages are broken down into components.

Figure 5 shows how often different adults were involved in interactions with children. Two items are noteworthy. First, the aides in the Unit-Based Program had very little interaction with children (3%), while Unit-Based teachers played a much larger role (33%). Second, children in the Cognitive Program had less total (although, as explained above, more individual) contact with teachers than did children in either of the other programs. Teachers in the Unit-Based Program did not differ greatly from Language Program teachers in the amount of time they spent interacting with children.

**Figure 5**

*Breakdown of Child-Adult Interaction—
Adults Interacting with Child*

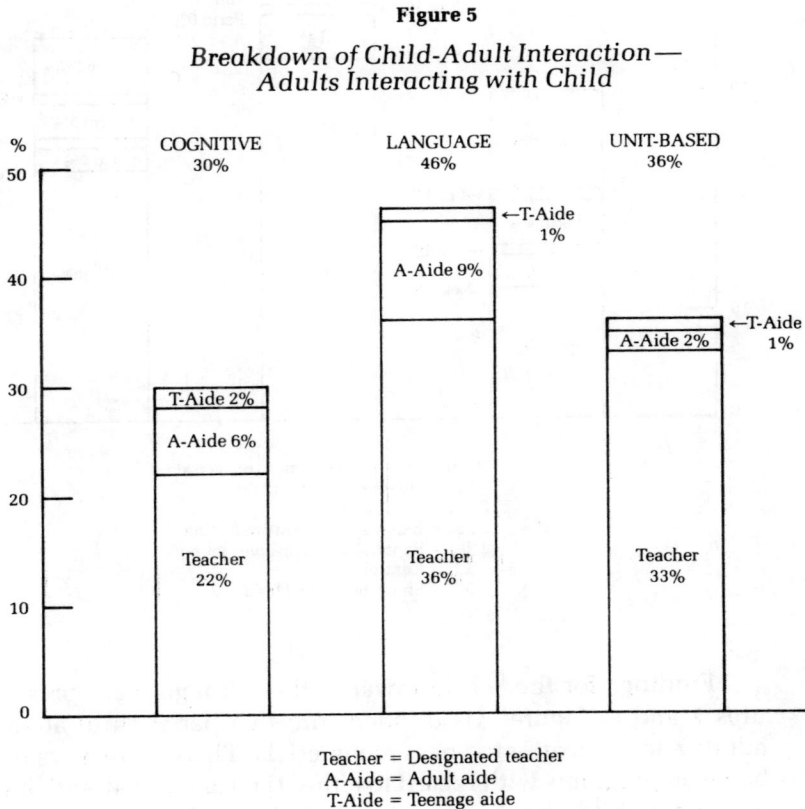

Teacher = Designated teacher
A-Aide = Adult aide
T-Aide = Teenage aide

The most frequently coded subcategory in the "adult behavior towards children" category was "telling"—direct, didactic teaching. As shown in figure 6, the Cognitive Program had the least amount of telling (12%); the Unit-Based Program had twice as much (23%) as the Cognitive Program; and the Language Program had three times as much direct teaching (33%) as the Cognitive Program. The extra child-adult interaction in the Language Program might have been due to the greater amount of direct teaching inherent in that approach. There were no other significant program differences in any of the remaining subcategories of adult behavior towards children. Again it should be noted that positive and negative feelings were defined as nonroutine, thus excluding the routine positive and negative reinforcement in the Language Program.

**Figure 6**

*Breakdown of Child-Adult Interaction—*
*Adult Behavior*

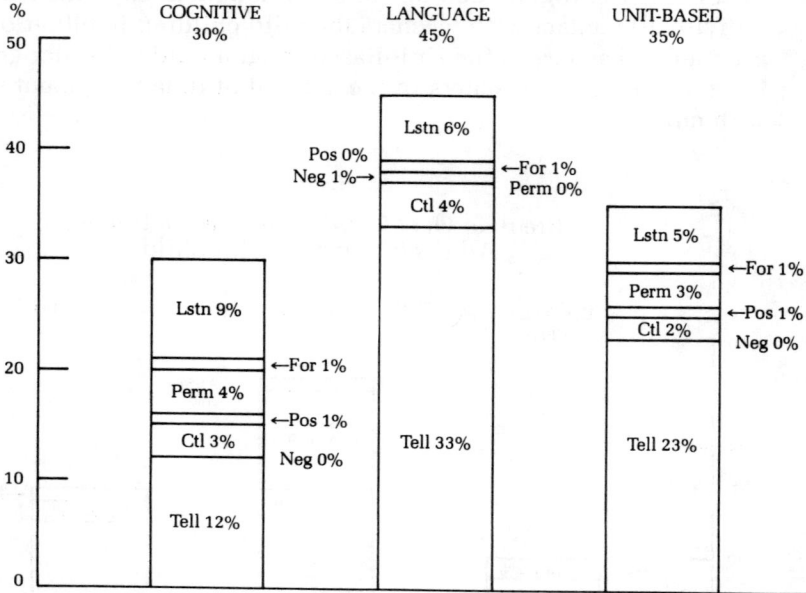

Lstn = Listen and question; conversation
For = Do something for child
Perm = Give permission
Pos = Expression of positive feeling
Neg = Expression of negative feeling
Ctl = Control
Tell = Show, tell, direct teaching

Findings for the "child toward other" category are presented in figures 7 and 8. Figure 7 is divided into two parts: child attentiveness to adults and child attentiveness to materials. There were no real differences between programs with regard to either type of child attentiveness. (There was more child attentiveness to adults in the Language Program simply because there was more child-adult interaction.) When children were by themselves, their attention to the materials before them appeared to wander about one-fifth of the time in the Cognitive Program and one-fourth of the time in the other two. Children's attention to adults was better, lapsing only 3% of their time or less in any program.

Findings for the "child-peer cooperation" category are presented in two parts in figure 8: observed child towards peers and peers towards observed child. Program differences in these categories appear to be attributable to the relative lack of child-child interaction in the Language Program. Across programs, observed children appeared to initiate and to cooperate in interactions in equal proportions. Peers, however, were seldom observed to initiate interaction with observed children, perhaps because peer initiations were too brief to be noticed. Noncooperation by peers was observed a bit more frequently than noncooperation by ob-

**Figure 7**

*Breakdown of Child Attentiveness to Adults and Materials*

a. Child attentiveness to adults

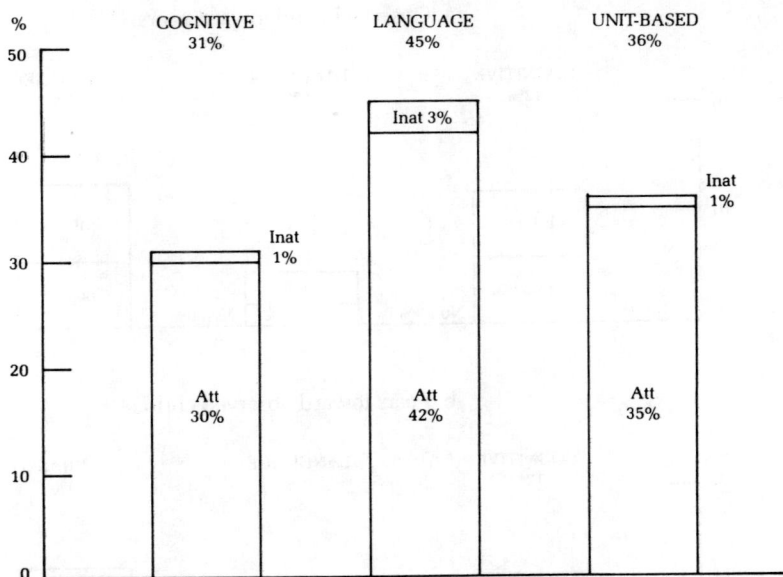

b. Child attentiveness to materials

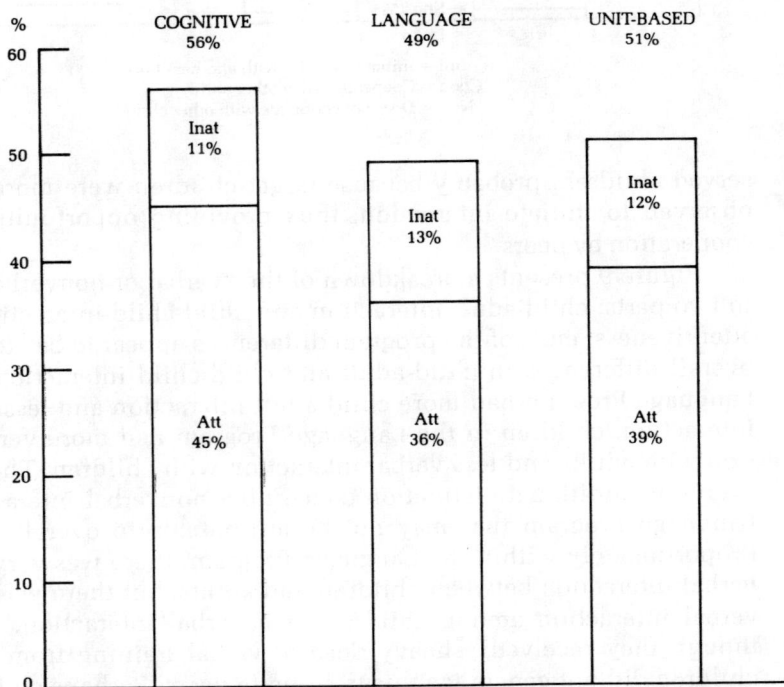

Inat = Inattentive
Att = Attentive

**Figure 8**

*Breakdown of Child-Child Interaction—*
*Child-Peer Cooperation*

a. Observed child toward peers

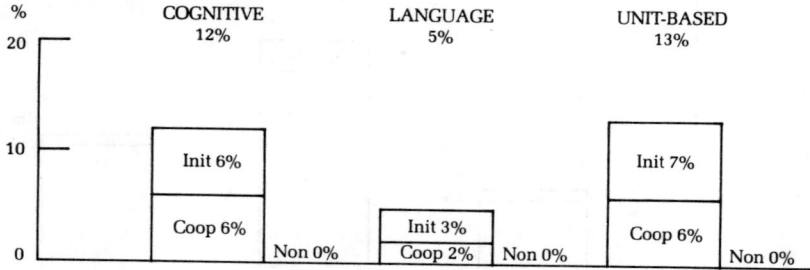

b. Peers toward observed child

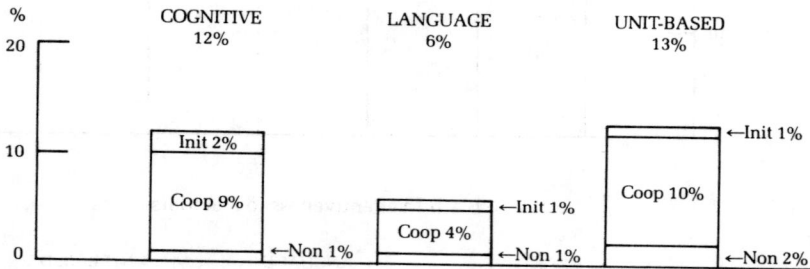

Init = Initiates activity with another child
Coop = Cooperates with other child
Non = Does not cooperate with other child

served children, probably because target children were more frequently observed to initiate interaction, thus providing opportunities for non-cooperation by peers.

Figure 9 presents a breakdown of the "verbal or nonverbal" category in two parts: child-adult interaction and child-child interaction. As with attentiveness, most of the program differences appear to be attributable to overall differences in child-adult and child-child interaction. Since the Language Program had more child-adult interaction and less child-child interaction, children in the Language Program had more verbal interaction with adults and less verbal interaction with children. There is, however, one additional distinction concerning nonverbal interaction in the Language Program that may not be attributable to overall differences. Proportionately within the Language Program, there was very little nonverbal interaction between children and adults, but there was more nonverbal interaction among children than verbal interaction. Thus, even though they received a heavy dose of verbal training from adults, the children did not generalize this training to peers. Perhaps children in the Language Program, receiving only verbal contact from adults, sought other types of contact (i.e., nonverbal) from their peers.

**Figure 9**

*Breakdown of Social Interaction—*
*Child's Verbal and Nonverbal Interaction*

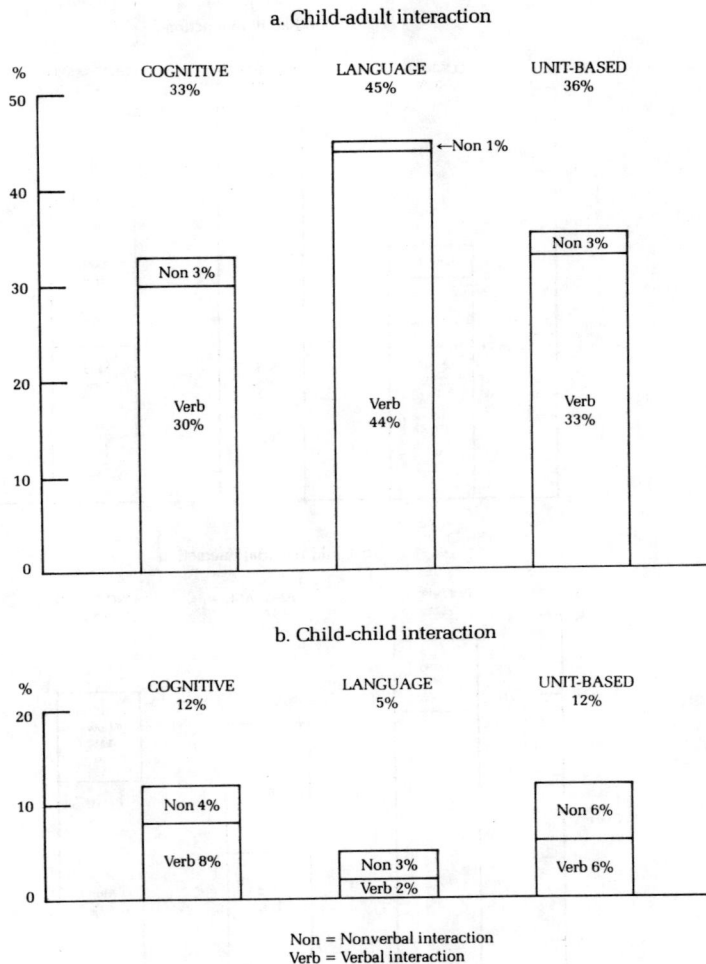

a. Child-adult interaction

b. Child-child interaction

Non = Nonverbal interaction
Verb = Verbal interaction

"Child's activity level" across the three major types of interactions is shown in figure 10. Proportionally, children were most active with other children (child-child), then by themselves (child-material), and then with adults (child-adult). In general, children in the Language Program were the most passive and children in the Cognitive Program were the most active, just as predicted by the curriculum descriptions. The findings of the Unit-Based Program, however, were less predictable. When a child in the Unit-Based Program was alone or with other children, his activity level tended to be relatively high (similar to that of children in the Cognitive Program). But when children in the Unit-Based Program were with adults, they became relatively passive, exceeding even children in the Language Program in this regard. It can be seen, then, that although the Unit-Based Curriculum describes a passive teacher and active children, the findings presented here suggest a more complex state of affairs.

**Figure 10**

*Breakdown of All Interactions—*
*Child's Activity Level*

a. Child-adult interaction

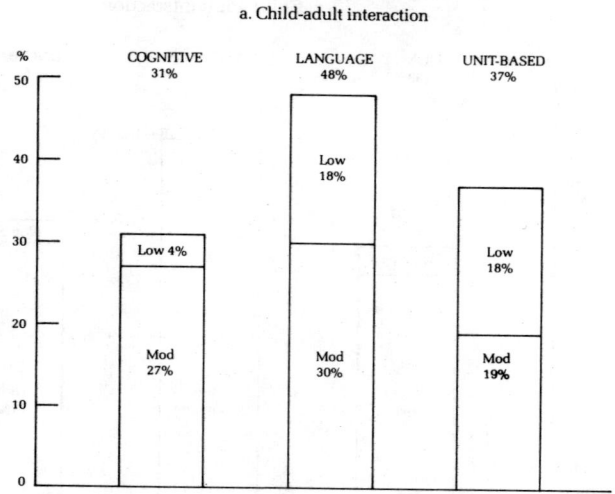

b. Child-material interaction

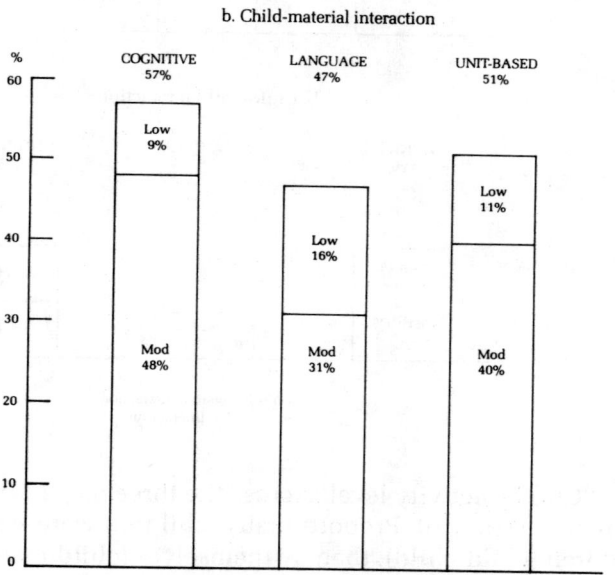

c. Child-child interaction

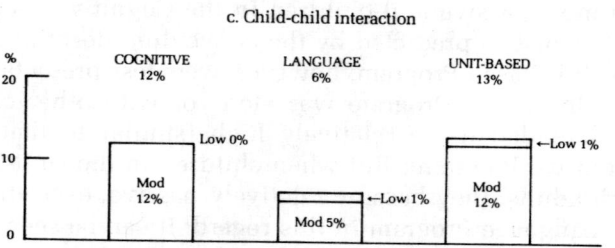

Low = Low activity level
Mod = Moderate activity level

Teachers in this program may have led more activities because they perceived economically disadvantaged children as needing more direct intervention. This intervention was counter-balanced, however, during free-play periods in which children were encouraged to adopt a more active role in their interactions with peers and materials.

Figure 11 depicts "nature of child's activity" by combining the three types of interaction. In all three programs, the most frequent type of interaction was the "convergent"; about half of the activities in the Cognitive and Unit-Based programs (48% and 56%, respectively) and almost three-quarters of the activities in the Language Program (72%) were coded in this category. Divergent and fantasy activities occurred about a fourth of the time in the Cognitive (16%) and Unit-Based (11%) programs, but scarcely at all in the Language Program (2%). There was more "work," i.e., socially useful activity, in the Cognitive (10%) and the Unit-Based (9%) programs than in the Language Program (4%). While this may be due to the fact that there were more materials with which to work in the first two programs, it is more likely attributable to the scheduling of extensive time periods during which such activities could take place.

It is interesting to examine the amount of child-defined activity (fantasy and divergent) as opposed to teacher-directed activity in each of the preschool programs since there were distinct curriculum expectations for such activities. As can be seen in figure 11, in both the Cognitive and Unit-Based programs the child chose and directed his own activities about a quarter of the time. In the Language Program, the child hardly ever chose or directed his own activities. This observed difference represents a point of considerable controversy in early childhood intervention programs. Proponents of the open framework (Cognitive) and child-centered (Unit-Based) models view self-chosen activity as important, in fact even crucial, to certain aspects of child development and therefore encourage such activity in their programs. Proponents of the programmed (Language) model see a child's time as much better spent in teacher-directed instructional activities.

PROSE findings are related to particular curriculum expectations in the next section.

## Summary of PROSE findings by preschool program

Table 5 is arranged to provide a quick summary of the PROSE findings for each of the preschool programs in the CD Project. Significant program differences were determined by the procedures described in appendix A. Since the PROSE was not developed specifically for the CD Project, i.e., with the three specific preschool programs in mind, it is important to interpret PROSE findings in terms of specific curriculum expectations. Two key questions should be addressed in such an interpretation: Did the operational programs represent the planned curricula? Were the dimensions which distinguish the curricula apparent in observed program differences? The first question is discussed here; the second question is addressed in the next section, "Validation of Curriculum Models by the PROSE."

**Figure 11**

*Breakdown of All Interactions— Nature of Child's Activities*

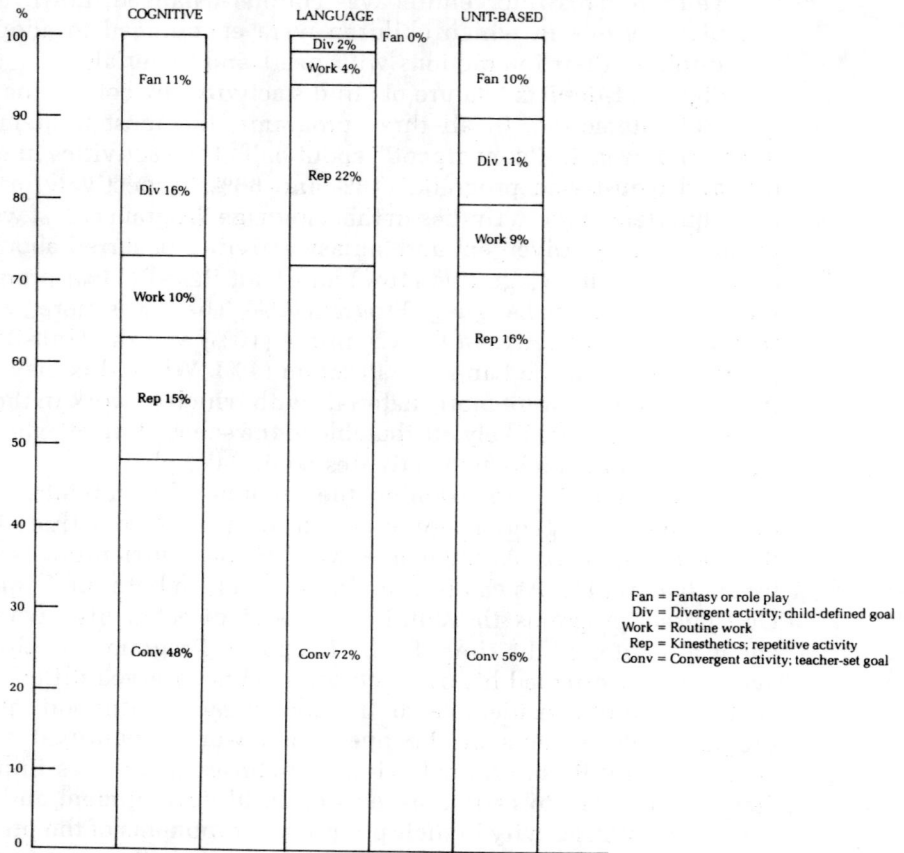

| % | COGNITIVE | LANGUAGE | UNIT-BASED |
|---|-----------|----------|------------|
| 100 | | Div 2%  Fan 0% | |
| | Fan 11% | Work 4% | Fan 10% |
| 90 | | | |
| | Div 16% | Rep 22% | Div 11% |
| 80 | | | |
| | | | Work 9% |
| 70 | Work 10% | | |
| | | | Rep 16% |
| 60 | Rep 15% | | |
| 50 | | | |
| 40 | | | |
| | Conv 48% | Conv 72% | Conv 56% |
| 30 | | | |
| 20 | | | |
| 10 | | | |
| 0 | | | |

Fan = Fantasy or role play
Div = Divergent activity; child-defined goal
Work = Routine work
Rep = Kinesthetics; repetitive activity
Conv = Convergent activity; teacher-set goal

**Language Program.** The Language Curriculum has been called an adult-centered approach to early childhood education. In this type of classroom, the adult's role is to be active, the child's passive, i.e., responsive to the adults. The adult is to transmit a body of information whose correctness is predetermined. Historically, such thinking represents the oldest approach to teaching in groups. The Language Curriculum sought to perfect this approach—to maximize its good points and make it as efficient as possible.

The PROSE findings showed that the Language Program differed from the Cognitive and, in some cases from the Unit-Based, in the following ways:

- more child-adult interaction
- less child-child interaction
- more adult attention to children in groups, less to individual children
- more direct teaching by adults
- more frequent passivity by children
- more teacher-directed activities
- fewer divergent activities or expressions of fantasy

**Table 5**

## Program Means and Differences on the PROSE

| CATEGORY | Mean % | High/Low % Difference | Cognitive | Language | Unit-Based |
|---|---|---|---|---|---|
| **Types of Interaction:** | | | | | |
| Child-adult | 38 | 12 | Low | High | Low |
| Child-material | 52 | — | | | |
| Child-child | 10 | 7 | High | Low | High |
| **Child Toward Adult:** | | | | | |
| Initiates | 3 | — | | | |
| Individual attention | 8 | 6 | High | Low | Low |
| In a group | 19 | 15 | Low | High | Middle |
| Attends to adult | 7 | — | | | |
| **Adult Involved:** | | | | | |
| Teacher | 30 | 13 | Low | High | High |
| Adult aide | 6 | 6 | High | High | Low |
| Teenage aide | 2 | — | | | |
| **Adult Behavior:** | | | | | |
| Listens, questions | 7 | — | | | |
| Do for child | 1 | — | | | |
| Gives permission | 2 | — | | | |
| Positive feeling | 1 | — | | | |
| Negative feeling | 0 | — | | | |
| Exerts control | 3 | — | | | |
| Tells, explains | 23 | 20 | Low | High | High |
| **Attention to Adult:** | | | | | |
| Attentive | 36 | 2 | Low | High | |
| Inattentive | 2 | — | | | |
| **Attention to Material:** | | | | | |
| Attentive | 40 | — | | | |
| Inattentive | 12 | — | | | |
| **Child Toward Peer:** | | | | | |
| Initiates | 5 | — | | | |
| Cooperates | 5 | 4 | | Low | High |
| Does not cooperate | 0 | — | | | |
| **Peer Toward Child:** | | | | | |
| Initiates | 1 | — | | | |
| Cooperates | 5 | 4 | High | Low | High |
| Does not cooperate | 1 | — | | | |
| **Mode of Child-Adult Interaction:** | | | | | |
| Verbal | 36 | 13 | Low | High | Low |
| Nonverbal | 2 | — | | | |
| **Mode of Child-Child Interaction:** | | | | | |
| Verbal | 5 | 7 | High | Low | High |
| Nonverbal | 3 | 5 | High | Low | High |
| **Child's Activity Level with Adults:** | | | | | |
| Low | 13 | 14 | Low | High | High |
| Moderate | 25 | — | | | |
| **Child's Activity Level with Materials:** | | | | | |
| Low | 12 | — | | | |
| Moderate | 41 | — | | | |
| **Child's Activity Level with Children:** | | | | | |
| Low | 1 | — | | | |
| Moderate | 10 | 7 | High | Low | High |
| **Nature of Child's Activities:** | | | | | |
| Fantasy | 7 | 9 | High | Low | High |
| Divergent | 10 | 12 | High | Low | High |
| Convergent | 59 | — | Low | High | |
| Work | 7 | 5 | High | Low | |
| Repetitive | 17 | — | | | |

NOTE: High, Middle and Low are noted only for differences with p <.05. (See appendix A for computational procedure.)

These findings constitute substantial evidence that the Language Program operated according to its planned curriculum.

**Unit-Based Program.** The child-centered model of the Unit-Based Curriculum may be seen historically as representing the first step in a revolt against adult-centeredness in education. Advocates of this approach assume that the child learns best from independent exploration of the environment, without adult intervention.

The PROSE findings showed that the Unit-Based Program differed from the Language Program in the following ways:

- less child-adult interaction
- more child-child interaction
- less adult attention to children in groups
- more nonverbal interaction between children
- more divergent activities and expressions of fantasy

As evidenced by these findings, there does seem to be a shift away from the adult-centered approach in the implementation of the Unit-Based Curriculum. Certainly more self-expression by children was observed in this program than in the Language Program.

**Cognitive Program.** Similar in some respects to the Unit-Based Curriculum, the Cognitive Curriculum nevertheless represents a further step in the revolt against adult-centeredness. Advocates of this approach assume that an emphasis on child activity and discovery need not entail a passive role for the adult in the educational process; that mental development proceeds through a child's active exploration of the physical environment as well as through supportive transactions with adults. In the Cognitive Program, the adult actively supports a child's development without being inappropriately directive. The adult asks questions and makes suggestions while taking into account the child's interest and readiness for an activity, i.e., his or her particular stage of development.

According to the PROSE, the Cognitive Program differed from the Language Program in all of the ways listed for the Unit-Based Program. In addition, the Cognitive Program differed from both the Language and Unit-Based programs in the following ways:

- more adult attention to individual children
- less direct teaching by adults
- less child passivity with adults
- fewer teacher-directed activities

These findings and those listed in the preceding paragraphs constitute considerable evidence that the Cognitive Program operated according to plan.

## Validation of curriculum models by the PROSE

Observations with the PROSE indicated that the three programs differed predictably from one another. First, they varied with respect to the relative roles played by the teacher and the child in the classroom. The Language Program was truly a programmed model in which teachers "initiated" and children "responded"; a group of children would listen to an adult's direct teaching and respond to her questions. Adults played a less directive role in both the Cognitive and Unit-Based programs. Teachers in the Unit-Based Program, however, did assume a more active role than is traditionally found in a child-centered model and, in fact, did significantly more direct teaching than did adults in the Cognitive Program. In both the Cognitive and Unit-Based programs, the lesser amount of teacher-child interaction relative to the Language Program was complemented by greater amounts of child-child interaction. Developing healthy peer relationships was an explicit goal of the child-centered or Unit-Based Curriculum. In the Cognitive Program such child interactions were one aspect of the open framework emphasis on active involvement with an environment which included, in part, one's peers.

The second broad area of program contrasts documented by the PROSE was the content of children's interactions, whether with other people or with materials. Children in the Language Program spent almost three-fourths of their time in convergent activity, i.e., mastering pre-academic skills defined by the teacher in a programmed and systematic manner. Convergent activity in the Language Program occupied the children one and a half times as much as in the other two programs. No fantasy and very little divergent activity were observed in the Language Program. By contrast, fantasy and divergent activity together accounted for over one-fourth and one-fifth of children's time in the Cognitive and Unit-Based programs, respectively. In the Cognitive Program, these activities reflected the emphasis of the open framework model on role play and "intrinsically motivated" active exploration as processes by which cognitive development occurs. In the child-centered Unit-Based Program, independent and creative activity was seen as central to the self-expression and growth of the whole child.

Thus, not only did the PROSE document that three distinct programs were in operation, it also indicated that each program represented one of the three basic curriculum models found in early childhood education.

# OBSERVATION OF CLASSROOM BEHAVIOR BY CONSULTANTS

In 1968 and 1969, 12 nationally recognized experts in child development and early childhood education accepted invitations to observe each of the three CD Project classrooms and record their observations. During their three-day visits, the consultants also held discussions with project staff and administrators and took part in conference sessions sponsored by the Ypsilanti Public Schools and held at Eastern Michigan University. The consultants were divided into four groups with each group visiting the preschool programs at a different time: spring or fall of 1968 or spring or fall of 1969. The consultants are identified below by area of specialization and institutional affiliation at the time of the observations.

*Spring 1968*

E. Kuno Beller, Intervention Research and the Role of Reinforcement; Temple University

Lawrence Kohlberg, Early Childhood Education, Cognitive and Moral Development; Harvard University

Todd Risley, Behavior Analysis; University of Kansas

*Fall 1968*

Marion Blank, Role of Language in Development; Hebrew University of Jerusalem

Courtney Cazden, Early Childhood Education, Role of Language in Early Childhood Education; Harvard University

Joseph Glick, Cognitive and Cross-Cultural Psychology; University of Minnesota

*Spring 1969*

J. McV. Hunt, Education of Disadvantaged; University of Illinois

Irving Sigel, Cognitive Development, Concept Development, and Cognitive Style; Merrill-Palmer Institute

Burton White, Early Childhood Education; Harvard University

*Fall 1969*

Edmund Gordon, Compensatory Education; ERIC Center for Disadvantaged

James Miller, Early Childhood Education; University of Illinois (National Laboratory for Early Childhood Education)

Leonard Sealey, Curriculum Development; Independent Consultant, New Haven, Sussex, England

Figure 12 shows the standard schedule that was followed for each of the four observation/consultation visits. It should be emphasized that the consultant observations were recorded *before* the information-exchange sessions.

The consultants represented a wide range of interests and theoretical positions on early childhood development and education. Individual reports tended to reflect the consultant's area of interest, whether it was cognition, learning, language development, or education of the disadvantaged child. As a result, there was a good deal of diversity in the observations recorded.

Following is a review of the observations reported by the consultants. The tone is conversational, reflecting the informal manner in which consultants were asked to record their observations. The information is organized by the four categories of their original records: program commonalities and then observations specific to the Language, Cognitive, and Unit-Based programs. Each section contains excerpts[13] of shared or contrasting observations which consultants made about various program

**Figure 12**

*Schedule for Observation/Consultation Visits*

| SUNDAY | MONDAY | TUESDAY | WEDNESDAY |
|---|---|---|---|
| Arrival<br><br>CD Project briefing (evening) | Observation 1[a]<br><br>Observation 2[a]<br><br>Observation 3[a]<br><br>Record observations using outline provided by CD Project staff[b] (evening) | Information-exchange sessions between consultants and CD Project administrative and teaching staff (High/Scope Camp) | Conference (Eastern Michigan University)—consultants lectured to CD Project staff and other interested individuals from the area<br><br>Departure (afternoon) |

[a]Daily preschool sessions were rescheduled and shortened from the normal 2½ hours to 1½ hours in order to allow all three programs to be observed in one day.

[b]The suggested report outline requested a statement of program commonalities and specific observations on each of the three preschool programs.

characteristics. The chapter concludes with a summary of consultant observations.

# Program commonalities

## Staff model

A high degree of staff involvement and commitment to program goals was fostered in each of the three CD Project programs. As stated in Weikart (1969): "The staff model is more important than the particular curriculum employed. While competent administrative direction and a good curriculum are important in achieving success, staff involvement is crucial. The staff model must allow each individual to be creatively involved in the total operation. In an almost romantic sense, the human involvement of concerned teachers and staff is the key element in program success. To achieve such involvement, a project must provide time for the staff to plan what they are going to do within the restrictions demanded by the curriculum, and it must provide for critical supervision by experienced personnel." (p. 25)

Risley: *In all three programs the teachers exhibited an amazing degree of enthusiasm and commitment to what they were doing. This statement also, to a lesser degree, includes the teacher aides. This project is remarkable for its talented teaching staff.*

Cazden: *All three programs have an impressive degree of teacher*

[13]Complete transcripts of consultant records are available upon request from the High/Scope Foundation.

enthusiasm and dedication, and teacher attention to the individual children. Someone quipped that what education needs is any cause for a widespread Hawthorne effect.[14] I wouldn't go that far. I'm sure there are things happening to children here that would make a difference under any circumstances. But the dedication and enthusiasm is probably the hardest characteristic to export outside of a program like this one, with teachers and researchers working together, national visibility, etc.

Blank: First I found that in all three classrooms the motivation of the teachers was extremely high. They had a lively atmosphere in the room. They were all very hard-working and very dedicated in spite of the obvious difficulties of the day.

Glick: One thing that seems common to all the groups is the tremendous amount of preparation involved in setting up the classroom for the kids. Clearly I have never seen so much preparation by a teacher before.

White: I think the overall quality of the six teachers was outstanding in this group, even for a research program where one would expect higher-quality teaching. I think the aides generally were also above average particularly in the language-based group, and I think this is of fundamental importance in an evaluation.

Sigel: The general impression one receives is of high interest and dedication of this group of professionals. The way the teachers in particular describe their own programs and commitments reflects a strong set of convictions that the programs in which they work are important and meaningful.

Gordon: The instructional staff is impressive. These young women come across as enthusiastic and committed to their work. They work hard and well with each other. They relate well to the children. They are warm, supportive, consistent and are unobstructive in their control of the learning environment.

Miller: I am most impressed with the general ability of the staff in the outlying positions, the supporting aides, and the leadership. One cannot help but be impressed with the task orientation, the high interpersonal regard and dedication that permeates all of the work observed.

## Use of language

One of the problems disadvantaged children are believed to face when entering school is a lack of language skills. Accordingly, each program in the CD Project attempted to develop these abilities within its particular curriculum framework. "Essential to the operation of all three curricula is the heavy use of language in the classroom. While the method of language training varies greatly, in all classes language is used extensively by the adults and is encouraged in the children." (Weikart, 1969, p. 18)

Sealey: Although the patterns of communication vary among the

---

[14]The Hawthorne effect is an outcome of a study which can be attributed to the increased attention received by subjects, rather than to the experimental treatment per se.

programs, ranging from the prescribed set used in the language training approach to the less-structured pattern of the Unit-Based Curriculum, speech is seen as the major means of interpersonal communication between teacher and child. In each case modes of expression as well as content have received careful consideration. Children appear to be learning speech patterns which not only help them to codify their various experiences but also enable them to communicate their experiences in the formal language that they will be required to use at a later stage both in and out of school. It was also evident that the richness and variety of the speech used in each of the programs had given rise to a considerable leap in the personal vocabularies of the majority of children.

Sigel: *All of them focus on language fluency and clarity, all accentuate number concepts and other verbal concepts of size and shape. The difference is in the dosing, the frequency, and the consistency with which these things are done.*

White: *As to the opportunity of these children to learn cognitive skills, especially those imbedded in language, I see little difference, despite the difference in style, between the Cognitive and Language curricula. On the other hand, the Unit-Based Curriculum falls far short of either of these, on the basis of the sample seen in this observation.*

Kohlberg: *It seemed to me that all three curricula stimulated language development but, perhaps from the viewpoint of spontaneous usage of language for cognitive and communicative purposes, the Unit-Based Program did the most.*

Glick: *Whereas the Language Program explicitly tries to ritualize speech patterns and the Cognitive Program attempts to expand but not extend what the children say, the teachers in the Unit-Based Program seem neither to extend nor expand the children's speech.*

## Working in groups and task completion

The ability to work in groups and to complete tasks was fostered in each of the programs. The Cognitive Program used a three-part sequence suggested by Sarah Smilansky (1968). "This sequence is planning, doing, and evaluating, and it has been formalized in the daily routine of the program as planning time, working time, and group meeting for evaluation." (Weikart, 1969, p. 10) The Language Program's use of highly structured group situations necessitated long periods of attention in groups. Developing social skills and the ability to function in groups as well as developing the ability to follow simple school routines and to complete tasks were goals of the Unit-Based Curriculum.

Sealey: *The second major commonality relates to the pressure exerted on children to reach closure, that is, to successfully complete a task or subtask; associated with this is the use of positive reinforcement. In each of the programs, despite their different styles, children were learning that there were single, "right" solutions to all problems, and that the achievement of the right solution would lead to some reward.*

Sigel: *All the programs have some emphasis on attention training, but again this varies, the most demanding being the Language Program followed by the Cognitive.*

Cazden: *All the programs get the children to focus and sustain attention and inhibit random, purposeless activity in favor of deliberate and planned action.*

### Home visits

The bi-weekly home visits made by CD Project teachers were aimed at engaging the mothers in the process of their children's education. Although the consultants did not have the opportunity to observe any of the home visits, a number of them speculated on the value of this aspect of the preschool programs.

Cazden: *Another real plus is obviously the home visits. I don't know about the effect on the mothers, but I believe the effect on teachers must be considerable, because the teachers must attend to individual children in planning for home visits. The third party is the child, and I wonder about the effect on him, not only through changes in what happens at home but also in his feelings about school and teacher. One boy in one group compared a game in school with the same game the teacher and he had played at home. Actually I was surprised not to hear more comments from children and teachers about the home visits.*

Glick: *In an experimental program you've got sort of a triple Hawthorne effect. The teachers feel they are on the spot, singled out in some way; the kids probably feel that way and the parents too, since they participate in the program through the home visits. I think it would be good to split your groups within programs into those who get home teaching and those who don't. I think in the future this will become a critical consideration.*

Hunt: *I find myself asking why these programs have produced larger IQ gains than any other programs of which I know. I find myself wondering if the home visits may not be the key to this gain, and I wish I knew more about them. It is extremely important to know if these home visits are making this kind of contribution. If they are, they promise not only to make the gains of the children more permanent but also, if the findings of Merle Karnes and the Peabody group are correct, to offer a basic enrichment to the lives of the parents themselves.*

# The Language Program

### Structure of the classroom and teacher orientation

The Language Training Curriculum was a programmed approach to preschool education. The emphasis was on teacher-initiated learning, and the program was closely structured to move children toward the attainment of program objectives. The extent of teacher involvement and program structure was the subject of observation and comments by many of the consultants.

White:[15] *In the Language Program, there was 24% [frequency of] self-initiated tasks vs. 76% [frequency of] teacher-initiated, but the [total amount of] time spent in self-initiated tasks was less than 7% [which] is really an incredibly small amount of time. [Thus] in the Language Program, 93% of the children's time is spent doing things the teachers want them to do.*

Gordon: *The learning climate in this classroom [Language Program] is more structured and teacher-directed. Teachers are warm and supportive but tend to demand more and are more task-oriented.*

Sealey: *It is understood that the teachers concerned with this program have limited degrees of freedom to make modifications. One modification which the teachers have made is the addition of semi-structured time. Although in fact, the activities which take place during this time are rigidly structured, they do provide much-needed opportunities for children to handle concrete objects.*

Sigel: *Here, as is self-evident, the program is predetermined, and the pacing, teacher strategy, and materials are all established by the teachers. The room is relatively simple and relatively barren compared to the Cognitive and Unit-Based classrooms. These are the rules of the game. I was impressed with the order, the quiet, the discipline, in this group. It is apparent that the teachers are in control and that the children are shaped up for the most part. They manifest the outward characteristics that make for a quiet, orderly classroom.*

Hunt: *The structured activities were obviously Bereiter-Engelmann in character. In fact the activities of these teachers could easily have been those of the teachers operating in this program in Champaign-Urbana.*

Glick: *The consistency of the stress of work was quite apparent throughout. The children were described as being "good workers" or doing "good work." There was a tremendous degree of work orientation verbally expressed and certainly carried through in the directed parts of the curriculum.*

Risley: *This program is characterized by a complete lack of unstructured activities. There is one apparently semi-structured activity, juice time; several activities that would be characterized as structured activities in the normal preschool; and a majority of activities that go completely off the structured end of the structured-unstructured scale of preschool activities.*

---

[15]White observed four children for five minutes each in each of the three programs and categorized their activities according to a system of social and nonsocial task behaviors. The percentages given by White refer to his calculations based upon this category system.

54

## Children's involvement

Despite the highly structured activities and task orientation of the Language Program, a number of consultants noted that the children appeared to be involved in the learning process and enjoying the program.

Sigel: *There is no question that the children are to a large degree involved in and moving along with the program.*

Hunt: *I got the impression that the children are not at all unhappy in their participation in the structured activities. They took a certain satisfaction in knowing the sounds of letters, in being able to make the separate sounds of the letters comprising a syllable of a word and then say them rapidly to uncover the word.*

Blank: *I think one of the important aspects of this program is the enormous motivation provided by the group setting. A large part is played by the teachers' enthusiasm, by group competition. "If so and so is going to do it, I'm going to do it," also plays a tremendously important role.*

## Social interaction

The emphasis in the Language Program was on mastery of academic skills. As a result, most of the classroom time was spent in structured groups. Social interaction with teachers and between children was limited. Limited interaction between peers was particularly noted by consultants. It is interesting that the juice period was mentioned as a time during which the lack of social interplay was most conspicuous. Not all the observers were aware that this period was planned by the teachers as a "quiet period" to give the children a rest period after the busy morning schedule.

Sealey: *The children seemed remarkably unaware of each other even while they were sitting close together around two tables. During a ten-minute period there were only two whispered attempts by children to communicate with each other.*

Glick: *But perhaps it's a very consistent model: that school time is mostly work time and we do certain things then, but there are off times too, and we do other things then. This was particularly apparent in the absolute silence of the rest of the period. Everybody leaned back and sort of said, "It's over at last, let's take a break. That was work, now it's rest."*

Cazden: *Not only the children, but the teachers seemed to be quiet at nonteaching times. I can well understand why you feel snacktime should be quiet, given the demands on everyone during the rest of the day. But this does convey a very different concept of school than in the other two programs. Is it only when none of the fours are present that the children are so quiet at transition times? I went out while they got their coats on and got into the bus: not a word. And the adults didn't initiate any conversation either. Or could this be the effect on both teachers and children of strict separation of teaching times from the rest of the school day?*

Blank: *First of all, I found that the children showed the least spontaneous movement and the least spontaneous conversation during times when they could have spoken to one another.*

Kohlberg: *Because of the lack of spontaneous interaction, it was difficult to detect what the relationship with the teachers was in the Language Training Program.*

## Positive reinforcement

Positive reinforcement was viewed as an essential part of the Language Program. Both "intrinsic" rewards (getting to leave the group first, allowing children to play teacher) and "extrinsic" rewards (stars and seasonal stickers on work, candy) were used. There was a good deal of verbal reinforcement written into the program to insure that a child was always praised immediately for a correct response. This aspect of the program was commented on by a number of observers.

Glick: *The constant administration of positive reinforcement, the teachers' styles, the vividness of their behavior were all quite striking. The dominant feature of this program as I saw it is that the teachers went absolutely out of their minds in an attempt to provide as much positive reinforcement for the kids as they possibly could.*

Risley: *The teachers exhibited an extremely high rate of praise and feedback to the children.*

Kohlberg: *Maintaining the children's attention is the major problem or difficulty in both the Cognitive and the Language programs. In the Language Program this is done very directly by using strong techniques to tell a child when he's not working hard, refusing to shake hands with him at the end of the session or touching and patting him to call his attention back if it wanders.*

Sealey: *It was interesting to note that the repetitive undiminished enthusiasm which the teachers displayed whenever a child completed a subtask appeared to leave many learners unmoved. Nevertheless, the expectation of reward was high. In one case a boy asked if he could have a cookie (the reward) before the actual lesson began.*

# The Cognitive Program

## Teacher involvement

The Cognitive Curriculum was an open framework approach to classroom organization. Children were assumed to learn through exploration and manipulation of the environment. The role of the teacher was to arrange the classroom to facilitate the learning of concepts by using the ongoing activities of the child to assess the child's level of ability and then introducing concepts at this level. This method of teaching was unique to the Cognitive Curriculum. Most of the consultants commented favorably on this feature, noting the individualized attention, the verbal interaction, and the interest of the children.

Beller: *My impression of the Cognitive Program was very much in line with my impression of the Unit-Based Program. The teachers are quite clearly oriented toward cognitive discrimination and learning. The cognitively oriented teacher asked more specific questions in relation to differences in size and distance, questions addressing themselves to identity of number, spatial relationships and seriation.*

Blank: *I think it would be very interesting in this program to evaluate the actual interchanges a child has with a teacher, both in terms of interchanges and amount of lesson time taken up in interchange, because the amount of one-to-one teaching time was quite considerable. There was a great deal of direct questioning on a one-to-one basis throughout and the children seemed interested and very relaxed with the teacher.*

Glick: *My overall impression of the Cognitive Curriculum is that there is a lot of stress placed on the verbal labeling of actions, directions and comparisons: same-different, big-little, etc. The curriculum people pretty much do what they say they are going to do, that is to use positive opportunities for the kids' own involvement in activities as the constant ground within which to imbed the various terms.*

Sigel: *The teachers seemed to grasp the principles of their curriculum and they utilized reinforcement procedures essentially in response to the children's intellectual performance. The program is one in which there is high teacher involvement, where the teacher seems to take the lead rather than just respond and where the teacher interjects herself continually.*

Miller: *I was impressed by the way in which the activities planned and implemented by the teachers were consistent with their theoretical orientation. As they become more comfortable with the inter-relationships of their instructional system, they will be able to take much greater advantage of the opportunities that constantly arise to work systematically at several levels of representation and operation.*

Hunt: *The teachers in the Cognitive Curriculum were forced to adapt their introduction of cognitively oriented activities to the intentional activities of youngsters as well as to their level of conceptual organization.*

Gordon: *One is very favorably impressed by the way that language usage, which receives heavy emphasis, grows out of the activities in which the children are involved.*

## Impulse control and daily routine

To increase attention span and help the child direct his own learning activities, the Cognitive Program stressed the need to adhere to a daily routine of which the children were aware. Teachers often verbalized the routine to the children, e.g., "What is the first thing we do?" or "What time is it now?" The consultants noted instances where the children were asked to wait for a new activity to begin or plan their next task. They agreed that this kind of planned delay probably added to the children's impulse control.

Blank: *A good deal of arbitrary delay was taught: waiting until everyone was seated, waiting until everyone had made their plans. This delay technique however, may be important in aiding the child to develop other cognitive skills.*

Glick: *The second feature is the rather consistent imposition of the lag, that is, the holding back of impulsive action contingent on something else. In some cases it was contingent on carrying through an activity the child had planned. In other cases it was contingent on the teacher's ordering of time in the classroom.*

Cazden: *At juice time, were the different levels of directions for the same-different concept planned or did it just happen that one teacher's group was asked to take two different cookies and the other teacher's group was asked to match her standard? I assume it was planned and I think it was excellent. During this juice time I also saw two other instances of impulse control via thinking and verbalizing before acting. (1) The teacher said, "Are you going to take the same or different? Tell me first." (2) Once the child had asked to pour the juice, the teacher held him to it, even when he wanted to switch to handing out the items that came earlier in the sequence.*

White: *"Prepare for action" comprised 7½% of the children's time in the Cognitive Curriculum compared to 3% in the Unit-Based and 0% in Language.* [White defined "prepare for action" as:] *To perform the socially prescribed activities or sequence of actions that a child carries out almost automatically due to previous experience and/or practice in order to prepare for something the child anticipates.*

## Planning, doing, evaluating

Smilansky's (1968) three-part sequence of planning, doing, and evaluating was incorporated into the routine of the Cognitive Program after her visit to the Perry Project as a consultant in the spring of 1964. During planning time, the child selected the area of the room where he would work and what he wanted to do there. During work time, he went to his chosen area and placed his tag on a "planning board;" if he left the area he took his tag with him. Finally, the group came back together to evaluate their work. Commenting on this system, the consultants all noted the children's compliance with the demands of the routine. Some felt that, for certain children, the freedom to change activities resulted in little task persistence.

Hunt: *I got the impression that these children were accustomed to an order of events, that they knew what a plan was, in at least a vague way, but the pressure to sustain any given plan was light.*

Gordon: *The form-coded name tag with the child's picture on it used in planning and in tracing the child is constantly and appropriately used. The child's name and the space he occupies in relation to other children and surroundings are creatively and consistently used.*

Cazden: *The procedure of changing one's symbol and moving from one activity to another really seems to work. I'm sure the teachers must have to be on their toes to watch each child and check up on anyone coming late to an area. It was very impressive to see one child, who was generally highly impulsive, spontaneously change his symbol before going over to another table. This enforced behavior of thinking before motorically acting out should be very important.*

Glick: *Coordinated with this attempt to label actions coherently are two other attempts. The first is the attempt to impose sequencing of activities which seemed to be a little bit ritualized. That is "First we do this and then we do this, and then we do this and then we do this," which may have been teaching the kids more about the peculiar quirks of the system than about the notion of sequence.*

Sealey: *Having made the decision to work at some activity, each child carried the picture which represented himself to the area in which he proposed to work. This much appeared readily accepted by the major-ity of children in the program, but they failed to understand that planning also implied a degree of persistence with a chosen task. The teachers appeared to accept that perambulation would be common. They insisted only that if the child changed areas, he first put his picture in the appropriate space.*

## The Unit-Based Program

### Teacher-child interaction

The Unit-Based Curriculum stressed the importance of teacher-pupil in-teraction in working with disadvantaged children. "The teacher can take cues from the children, but often has to be the instigator of new ideas, especially in role play. Eventually it is hoped that the child will begin spontaneous conversation with the teacher, expressing needs or giving cues the teacher can expand upon." (McClelland et al., 1970, p. 2) The con-sultants differed in their views on the effectiveness of the teachers' inter-actions with the children during discovery time. While some felt the teachers were being effective, others commented on the lack of intensive interaction.

Kohlberg: *The best relationships between children and teachers seemed to be in the Unit-Based Program. The relationship seemed good in the sense of the children liking and trusting the teachers.*

Blank: *The teachers paid very good attention to the individual re-sponses of the children. I think in watching the children that in spite of their overall very good attitude when they are left on their own they do* relatively little, and their activity did not indicate any high level of symbolization. Many of the children just randomly started sorting things. The teachers intervened, directing their attention to a particular object or set of circumstances.

Beller: When the Unit-Based teachers raised questions, they were more clearly directed toward labelling objects, the content of experience and behavior rather than its cognitive structure and interrelationships. The questions of the teachers in the Unit-Based Program appeared to be more oriented toward increasing vocabulary and expanding general knowledge in relationship to something that the child was playing with at the time.

White: There is more teacher control in the Unit-Based Program than might have been predicted. For example, in calculating the frequency of self- and teacher-initiated tasks compared to the total time spent on each kind, you find that the children initiated tasks 61% of the time while the teachers initiated tasks only 40% of the time, but the total time spent on those tasks was 43% for self-initiated and 57% for teacher-initiated. This means that the children initiated more tasks themselves in the Unit-Based Program but stuck longer with the ones that the teachers initiated.

Miller: In the Unit-Based Curriculum we see the locus of structure being entirely within the teacher—implicit, private, and in the main, un-communicable. The danger in such a state of affairs is that one must rely upon charisma—something magical about the adult-child relationship within an educational setting which is hardly transferable to other people with the same responsibility.

Sigel: It is impossible for the teachers to be involved in all of these [discovery time] activities, and the teachers in this group tended to be more like participant-observers, relatively speaking, than those in the other two groups. In this type of arrangement, then, the teacher's behavior is less continuous, since she is shifting sporadically from child to child. In the discovery period, she deals primarily with each child individually but in a relatively passive manner, and then there is little follow up or follow through.

Hunt: I observed more child-to-child talk in the Unit-Based Cur-riculum than in either of the other two but what was missing in a large share of these activities was talk between teachers and children. What I missed was any evidence of teacher intervention to help children cope with the group process of socialization, with the business of sharing, taking turns, respecting the rights of others, good manners, etc.

Risley: The children in the afternoon group exhibited remarkably complex social interactions which were for the most part independent of the teachers' facilitation. To a large extent their interactions with the children were in the form of moving about and commenting on what the children were doing and throwing in an occasional suggestion or provid-ing new materials for the children's activities.

Sealey: The daily discovery time provides ongoing opportunities for the teachers to make differentiated responses based upon their observa-tions of the children at work.

## Peer interaction

The development of social skills was one of the goals of the Unit-Based Program. Peer interaction and spontaneous conversation were encouraged, and the presence of this kind of interaction was commonly noted by the consultants.

Kohlberg: *First dramatic play—a few of the children in the Unit-Based Program enacted sustained cooperative goals—husband-wife and so on. Part of the reason for the greater capacity for dramatic play in the Unit-Based Program was the "let's pretend" attitude of the teachers as reflected in the group activities.*

Risley: *In the afternoon group [Unit-Based], because of the emphasis on unstructured activities, social interaction of the teachers and children seemed much more pleasant for each, with the exception of three or four children who seemed to demand special planning on the part of the teachers. The children in the afternoon group exhibited remarkably complex social interactions which were for the most part independent of the teachers' direct facilitation.*

Blank: *I found this the liveliest classroom in terms of the children's spontaneous activity, their talking and interacting with each other.*

Sigel: *The social interaction varies, being particularly low in the Cognitive and Language programs relative to the Unit-Based.*

Sealey: *The children also interacted quite freely with each other, using complete sentences in their conversations. Some children have achieved a fair level of sophistication in this respect. For example, a child who was playing with one of the two tills in the toy store asked her boy partner who was working with the other till if she could have some of the money. He gave her a number of token coins, to which she responded, "Aren't you going to give me any more?"*

## Discovery time and task persistence

The emphasis in the Unit-Based Program was on "learning by experience," or "discovery through play." The children were allowed freedom within certain limits to choose activities, move from one activity to another, or engage in social interactions and role play. A number of observers observed that the children actually exhibited a good deal of task persistence during this period, while others noted a lack of sustained activity.

Beller: *The child's fantasy life should be emphasized and meaning made of his overt behavior. Although I did not find evidence of this in the written materials or in the teacher behaviors within the Unit-Based Program, there is some evidence of its effect in that program, for the children in the Unit-Based Program expressed their problems much more clearly in spontaneous play activities than I was able to find in the other two programs.*

Kohlberg: *I saw more sustained attention to a task in the Unit-Based Program than I did in the other two. Why the Unit-Based Program's pupils show more sustained attention to tasks, I'm not clear. This came primarily in the free activities rather than during group sessions. Nevertheless, there was more opportunity for individual construction and working with individual cognitive puzzles and materials in the Unit-Based than in the Cognitive Program.*

Sigel: *The Unit-Based Program is characterized by a greater amount of individualized play with some relatively long play activities where one child may be working consistently and persistently with a puzzle while other children are playing with large motor objects. [However] since this group is less structured than the other two, there was more movement around the room. Children did not confine their activities to single areas, although some effort was made by at least one of the aides to maintain such order.*

Hunt: *Inasmuch as free play gives children an opportunity to follow completely their own intentions, I saw at least three children in their own intended activities for longer periods of time than any other children I observed during the day. Some children did have prolonged periods of self-directed activity, but others jumped from thing to thing without any such control.*

Sealey: *Although a number of children perambulated from one activity to another, each exhibited a degree of task persistence.*

White: *The nontask category doesn't really figure here except in the Unit-Based Program, where there is some rambling around; it's seventh ranked, 4% of all real time.*

## Summary of consultants' observations

The program commonalities noted by the observers were features that the three curricula shared as major goals. It is significant that these common characteristics were apparent to the consultants during their visits because they were not informed of the research or individual curriculum goals until after their observations had been recorded. All the consultants commented upon the high degree of staff enthusiasm and commitment to both the project and the children. There was general agreement that language development was emphasized, although the method and degree of this emphasis differed according to the curriculum model. Sustained attention and task persistence were also noted as common goals, although again both the extent and success of this focus were found by observers to differentiate programs. Finally, although home visit sessions were not actually observed, several consultants commented upon the potential importance of this common program component.

Observers agreed that the high degree of structure in the Language Program was consistent with the Bereiter-Engelmann model. Children were seen as primarily engaged in teacher-initiated activities. Despite this extensive teacher-directedness however, several consultants commented that the children seemed involved, motivated, and satisfied with their participation in the learning process. The clear division between work and nonwork time was noted by many observers to result in a lack of spontaneous social interaction between teachers and children, as well as among the children themselves. Positive reinforcement, an important feature of this curriculum, was found to be employed effectively by the teachers.

In the Cognitive Curriculum, the role of the teacher was viewed as one of high involvement, with an emphasis on adapting Piagetian concepts to the level of the child's cognitive development. Several consultants noted that delays were built into the daily routine and individual activities in order to extend the children's ability to control impulses. A three-part sequence of planning, doing, and evaluating was used to develop task persistence and temporal awareness, but observers differed in evaluating the success with which this procedure achieved these goals.

Consultants differed in interpreting the role ascribed to teachers in the Unit-Based Program. Some saw teachers as being relatively passive and not intervening in the children's individual tasks or social interactions; others noted that the children were quite dependent upon the teachers to structure their activities and direct their attention. There was general agreement that this program had the highest level of spontaneous social interaction, both between the children and adults and among the children themselves. Task persistence and sustained attention were found by some observers to be surprisingly high in the Unit-Based Program given its relative lack of structure. Other consultants did note, however, that some children had difficulty remaining with a single task for an extended period of time.

In conclusion, the independent observations of this group of consultants support the claim that this study compared preschool programs which were operationally, as well as theoretically, different. While they differed to some extent in their views of how closely or effectively the three program models were followed, the observers did basically agree that three distinct curricula were being implemented in the CD Project.

# HOME VISIT REPORTS

Every two weeks, teachers made home visits to each child in the three programs. Each teacher was responsible for approximately half the children in her classroom, so that the same teacher visited each child throughout the year. There were 12 home visits per child per year for two years, i.e., a total of 24 home visits per child for the duration of the program.

After completing each visit, teachers filled out a Home Visit Report (HVR) consisting of 22 items (see appendix B). Because there was only one teacher for each visit, there was no opportunity to collect reliability data on teachers' answers to HVR questions.

The HVRs reported on three aspects of the home visits: the setting, maternal behavior, and the curriculum. First, the mechanics or "setting" of each visit was described, including such variables as the length of the visit, the number of other children and adults present, the length of time the mother participated, whether or not the mother and child were prepared for the visit, evidence that the mother and/or child had used the materials left by the teacher on the previous visit, and so forth. Second, the teacher rated the mother's behavior during the visit on a number of subjective personality dimensions (e.g., active versus passive reaction to program, strictness versus permissiveness of mother's relationship with child, openness versus closedness of mother's relationship with teacher, rigidity versus flexibility of mother's personality) and on some more objective behavioral dimensions (e.g., amount of information mother communicated to child, mother's use of positive and negative motivation with child, extent to which mother questioned the child, extent to which mother copied teacher's teaching methods). Third, each teacher listed her goals for the child during that session, and explained in detail the particular educational activities that occurred during the home visit, i.e., the "curriculum operation" during the session. HVRs for the three programs were compared on these three aspects of the home visits. Differences between the three programs with respect to setting, maternal behavior, and curriculum operation are discussed below.

## The setting of the home visits

For each child, three reports were selected from each of the four semesters of preschool attendance (FEY, SEY, F2Y, S2Y) as representative of the total number of reports (24). Discarding the first and last visit of each year as atypical (i.e., first visits often involved filling out forms while last visits were sometimes special parties or trips), fall semester reports were chosen closest to the beginning of the school year and spring semester reports were chosen closest to the end of the school year. This resulted in 12 HVRs which were then averaged for each child to assess the home visit setting.

Sixteen variables describing the home visit setting were derived from the answers to items 1-8 and 13 of the HVRs. The average HVR scores on these 16 variables were then analyzed using one-way analyses of variance comparing treatment groups. Results of these analyses are presented in table 6.

Examining the data, one is first struck by the similarity of the home visit setting across the three groups:

- Sessions in the home generally lasted close to an hour and a half, with mothers most often being present in the home for more than 95% of the visits.
- There was frequently at least one child in addition to the sample child present in the home (generally a sibling, but sometimes a cousin or neighbor) and these other children participated in the home visit activities approximately half the time.
- Mothers and children were almost always ready for the teacher and had a work space prepared.
- The mothers rarely used the home visit sessions to raise personal problems with the teachers.

**Table 6**

*Home Visit Setting Variables*

| Variable | Cognitive (N=11) | | Language (N=15) | | Unit-Based (N=15) | | F Ratio |
|---|---|---|---|---|---|---|---|
| | Mean | S.D. | Mean | S.D. | Mean | S.D. | |
| Length of visit (in minutes) | 87.9 | 7.21 | 86.6 | 3.10 | 87.9 | 6.57 | <1 |
| Was mother in home?  1 = no  2 = yes | 1.9 | 0.20 | 1.9 | 0.13 | 1.8 | 0.27 | <1 |
| Length of time mother in home (if in home), in minutes | 87.0 | 6.67 | 84.6 | 4.13 | 82.4 | 11.57 | <1 |
| Did mother participate in teaching process?  1 = no  2 = yes | 1.8 | 0.19 | 1.8 | 0.31 | 1.5 | 0.37 | 3.54* |
| How long did mother participate (if she participated), in minutes | 66.1 | 20.32 | 60.3 | 16.11 | 64.0 | 20.73 | <1 |
| Were any other adults present?  1 = no  2 = yes | 1.7 | 0.22 | 1.4 | 0.28 | 1.4 | 0.35 | 4.84* |
| Number of adults present (including mother but not including teacher) | 2.3 | 0.58 | 1.6 | 0.50 | 1.5 | 0.54 | 7.08** |
| Number of children present (including preschooler) | 2.5 | 1.00 | 2.3 | 0.78 | 2.7 | 1.34 | 1.92 |
| Did children other than preschooler participate in teaching?  1 = no  2 = yes | 1.4 | 0.44 | 1.5 | 0.24 | 1.4 | 0.29 | <1 |
| Were mother and child ready?  1 = no  2 = yes | 1.9 | 0.98 | 1.9 | 0.13 | 1.8 | 0.18 | <1 |
| Did mother prepare a place for teacher?  1 = no  2 = yes | 2.0 | 0.10 | 1.9 | 0.11 | 1.9 | 0.12 | 1.39 |
| Did mother find other activities to occupy her time?  1 = no  2 = yes | 1.3 | 0.37 | 1.3 | 0.32 | 1.4 | 0.30 | <1 |
| Did mother ask questions about learning materials?  1 = no  2 = yes | 1.5 | 0.32 | 1.3 | 0.32 | 1.5 | 0.35 | 1.04 |
| Did mother raise personal problems?  1 = no  2 = yes | 1.0 | 0.06 | 1.0 | 0.09 | 1.0 | 0.09 | <1 |
| Mother implemented teacher's suggestions between visits[a]  1 = not at all  7 = very much | 5.5 | 3.13 | 3.5 | 2.39 | 4.7 | 3.57 | 1.49 |
| Child used teacher's materials between visits[a]  1 = not at all  7 = very much | 4.3 | 2.29 | 2.3 | 1.30 | 3.3 | 2.78 | 2.43 |

*p<.05.
**p<.01.
[a]According to mother's report to teacher

■ Mothers in all three groups asked questions about the learning materials approximately half the time, and there was evidence that mothers implemented teachers' suggestions and that children used materials between visits to a moderate degree.

Although the means on these last two between-visit variables were highest in the Cognitive and lowest in the Language group, these group differences were not significant.

Means on three of the 16 home visit setting variables, however, were significantly different across the three groups. Mothers in the Cognitive and Language programs participated in the home teaching sessions more often than mothers in the Unit-Based Program. In addition, adults other than the mothers were more often present during Cognitive Program visits, although it is not known whether they watched and participated or took care of other children present, which would have allowed the mother to participate more. A number of explanations may be offered for the greater participation of Cognitive and Language mothers in comparison to Unit-Based mothers. Perhaps, in order for mothers to become involved, they need to be able to see concretely what the educational "program" for their children actually is. This in turn gives them a more concrete idea of what their role can be, particularly when teachers model or explain to parents specific activities which they can do with their children. The Cognitive and Language programs, in contrast to the Unit-Based, appeared to have more clearly articulated "programs" and might have been able to define more explicit activities for mothers to do with children (e.g., role-play and classification games, language drill). In addition, the commitment of the Unit-Based Program to the child's freedom to initiate his or her own "learning by playing" extended to the activities in the home visit sessions; this philosophy may have resulted in less opportunity for direct parental involvement.

It is also interesting to note that the analysis of the PROSE data showed less interaction with aides and more with teachers in the Unit-Based Program than in the other two programs. Perhaps this finding, together with the less frequent involvement of mothers during home visits, suggests a certain "proprietariness" on the part of the Unit-Based teachers. That is, they may have viewed the children in the program as "their children" and been reluctant to have others (aides, mothers) usurp their teaching roles. Alternatively, the same relative vagueness about program goals and adult roles could have limited the involvement of both aides and mothers in activities with the children.

Apart from differences in maternal involvement, the setting within which home visits occurred did not differ across programs. This is as it should be, for only if these contextual aspects of program operation are constant across the three curricula can outcome differences be attributed to differences in curriculum models.

## Maternal behavior ratings during the home visits

As described above, the mother's behavior during each visit was rated by the teacher on a number of subjective and relatively objective dimensions. Because no reliability data can be obtained on these maternal ratings, the results from the subjective personality dimensions will not be dealt with further. Only those items where teachers rated mothers on concrete observable behaviors during the home visits are analyzed here.

Six variables on which maternal behavior was rated were derived from items 10-A through 10-D of the HVRs. For each of these variables, mothers were rated by teachers as showing the behavior anywhere from "1" (very little) to "7" (a great deal). For each mother, the three reports for FEY, SEY, and S2Y were averaged separately, and then analyzed to examine group differences at the beginning of the project, and after one and two years of home visits.

Table 7 presents the results of a repeated measures analysis of variance of maternal ratings comparing groups from fall to spring of the entering year. No significant group or trial main effects or interaction effects were found. Thus, mothers in the three groups appear very similar to each other at the beginning and the end of their children's first year in preschool. Further, when all groups were combined, mothers' behavior did not change significantly from the fall to the spring of the entering year.

Table 8 presents the results of a repeated measures analysis of variance of maternal ratings comparing groups from the fall of the entering year to the spring of the second year, i.e., the duration of the program. Again there were no significant main effects, indicating that mothers in each group were similar to each other over the course of the project, and that mothers did not change significantly over the two years when the three groups were combined.

The two significant Group-by-Trials interactions (feedback requests and expansiveness) were further analyzed by post-hoc comparisons. It was found that Cognitive group mothers made significantly larger gains on these two variables than mothers in the Language and Unit-Based groups. Encouraging mothers to address more informational questions to their children was consistent with Cognitive curriculum goals. However, this finding of a change in maternal behavior should be interpreted with caution since no significant group differences on these two variables appeared at either the beginning or the end of the two-year preschool period.

In summary, maternal behavior during the home visits was quite similar for all three treatment groups and, with the exception of increased questioning of the child in the Cognitive group, mothers did not evidence any changes in their behavior during the two years of home visits. While these results may reflect the similarity in the backgrounds of all the mothers and/or the uniform impact of a home visit program for this group as a whole, the lack of significant findings may be attributable to the assessment procedure. Even though mothers were being rated on observable behaviors, there are no reliability data to indicate whether teachers were basing these ratings on shared standards or individual bases.

## Curriculum operation variables during the home visits

The educational activities that occurred during home visits were expected to be consistent with each of the three curriculum models and were

**Table 7**

*Maternal Ratings During First Year*

| Variable | Cognitive (N=10) | | Language (N=13) | | Unit-Based (N=15) | | Group Main Effect F Ratio | Trials Main Effect F Ratio | Group by Trials Interaction F Ratio |
|---|---|---|---|---|---|---|---|---|---|
| | FEY Mean | SEY Mean | FEY Mean | SEY Mean | FEY Mean | SEY Mean | | | |
| To what extent did mother copy teacher's teaching methods? | 2.8 | 3.3 | 3.5 | 3.2 | 3.0 | 3.3 | $<1$ | $<1$ | $<1$ |
| How much general and specific information did mother communicate to child? | 2.7 | 3.1 | 3.2 | 2.7 | 2.5 | 2.4 | $<1$ | $<1$ | $<1$ |
| Did mother use positive motivation? | 4.9 | 4.0 | 4.8 | 4.3 | 4.1 | 4.3 | $<1$ | 2.48 | 2.76 |
| To what extent did mother ask child for information? (Feedback requests) | 2.2 | 2.2 | 2.8 | 2.3 | 2.2 | 2.3 | $<1$ | $<1$ | $<1$ |
| To what extent did mother use positive motivation and ask for information? (Expansive) | 2.7 | 2.6 | 3.2 | 2.6 | 2.5 | 2.6 | $<1$ | 1.99 | 1.22 |
| To what extent did mother use negative motivation and communicate general information to child? (Restrictive) | 4.5 | 4.1 | 4.5 | 4.1 | 3.7 | 4.1 | $<1$ | $<1$ | 1.97 |

NOTE: FEY = Fall, Entry Year of Preschool
SEY = Spring, Entry Year of Preschool

**Table 8**

*Maternal Ratings Over Two Years*

| Variable | Cognitive (N=10) | | Language (N=13) | | Unit-Based (N=15) | | Group Main Effect F Ratio | Trials Main Effect F Ratio | Group by Trials Interaction F Ratio |
|---|---|---|---|---|---|---|---|---|---|
| | FEY Mean | S2Y Mean | FEY Mean | S2Y Mean | FEY Mean | S2Y Mean | | | |
| To what extent did mother copy teacher's teaching methods? | 2.8 | 4.6 | 3.5 | 3.4 | 3.0 | 3.2 | <1 | 1.41 | 3.11 |
| How much general and specific information did mother communicate to child? | 2.7 | 4.0 | 3.2 | 2.9 | 2.5 | 2.6 | 1.03 | <1 | 3.15 |
| Did mother use positive motivation? | 4.9 | 4.8 | 4.8 | 4.2 | 4.1 | 4.3 | <1 | <1 | <1 |
| To what extent did mother ask child for information? (Feedback requests) | 2.2 | 3.3 | 2.8 | 2.7 | 2.2 | 2.5 | <1 | 2.40 | 4.58* |
| To what extent did mother use positive motivation and ask for information? (Expansive) | 2.7 | 3.7 | 3.2 | 3.1 | 2.5 | 2.5 | <1 | <1 | 3.27* |
| To what extent did mother use negative motivation and communicate general information to child? (Restrictive) | 4.5 | 5.0 | 4.5 | 3.9 | 3.7 | 4.2 | 1.11 | <1 | 2.87 |

NOTE:  FEY = Fall, Entry Year of Preschool
S2Y = Spring, Second Year of Preschool

*p<.05.

designed to parallel the activities that occurred each day in the classroom. Demonstrating that home visit activities were, in fact, based on three distinct curricula is central to the premises upon which this curriculum demonstration study is based. Because of the importance of documenting differences in curriculum operation during the home visits, the activities reported in all 24 HVRs per child were analyzed.

Twenty-five variables were derived from item 16 of the HVR, in which the teacher provides a "description of activities" occurring during each home teaching session. Table 9 describes each of these variables. The 24 HVRs for each child were scored according to these 25 variables, such that 1 = Activity Not Done and 2 = Activity Done during each visit. An average score was then computed for each variable across the 24 visits. Inter-coder reliability was established by having two coders independently code 15 HVRs, five for each of the three curricula. Percentages of agreement, computed with Cartwright's (1956) alpha, are reported for each variable in table 10.[16] For all variables, reliability was high, ranging from 86.7% to 100% with an average inter-coder agreement across the 25 variables of 96.5%. However, it should be noted that for a few categories (i.e., TRUNIT, TRACAD, TRREL, SOCMAN, and SOCEGO) the activity was agreed upon as "done" only two times or less out of the possible 15 home visits. Thus, the high inter-coder reliability for these variables is based primarily on "not" seeing an activity, rather than seeing an activity (such as reading), and interpreting its content in the same way.

In addition, the teacher making each home visit was also noted in order to address the criticism that this study compared teachers rather than curricula. Children's average scores (across 24 visits) for each of the 25 variables were thus coded according to the program and the teacher or teachers[17] making the home visits for a particular child. It was hypothesized that the home visit activities of children in different programs would be significantly different, whereas the activities of children in the same program but with different teachers (or teacher pairs) would not. In other words, a child's treatment should be defined by the program he or she was in, rather than by his or her particular teacher(s) within that program.

Group differences in home visit activities were first analyzed by activity "areas," i.e., visual-motor, language, object identification, reading, numbers, field trips, and social-emotional. Table 11 presents the results of one-way analyses of variance comparing groups for each activity area. Six of seven areas showed a significant group effect; only the visual-motor area did not. Table 12 presents the significant results of post-hoc comparisons on group differences in activity areas. The Cognitive Program, in comparison with the other two, had the least amount of reading. The Language Program had more reading and number activities

---

[16]If both coders scored the same activity as being "done" or "not done" during a given home visit, this was considered an agreement in coding. If one coder scored an activity as being "done" while the other coder scored this same activity as "not done," this constituted a coding disagreement.

[17]Many children in the Cognitive and Language programs had a different home visit teacher in the first and second years because of changes in the teaching staff. In these cases, the average score for each variable across the 24 visits actually represents the score for a teaching "pair" rather than an individual teacher.

**Table 9**

*Variables for Description of Home Visit Activities*

| Variable | Description |
|---|---|
| | VISUAL-MOTOR (e.g., cutting, pasting, drawing, tracing, puzzles, Frostig visual-motor materials, large motor games, building with blocks, stringing beads, clay, small tools) |
| VMOWN | For own sake; no explicit rationale offered for activity; to learn to hold scissors, crayons, etc. correctly; to emphasize visual-motor coordination and development; Frostig puzzles assembled with increasing number of pieces. |
| VMUNIT | As part of unit, e.g., to make Christmas decorations or Halloween masks; folding "letters" to give to the mailman for unit on community helpers. |
| VMACAD | To emphasize pre-academic skills, e.g., learning to write letters, numbers, etc.; printing sounds of letters; making scrapbook with rules and identity statements for items on each page; connecting dots by number; coloring by number; language drill such as identity statements about body parts that child cuts and pastes; tracing and drawing lines as prerequisite to writing letters and numbers; motor activity while singing the alphabet song. |
| VMREL | To emphasize relations, e.g., seriation by drawing and cutting out circles of graduated sizes; classification using the "vehicle" or "clothing" puzzle; spatial representation by drawing the body; motor encoding by acting out how to drink with a cup and saucer; spatial relations in playground games; motor encoding through acting out different roles; cutting out "cookies" of graduated sizes from playdoh; seriation of sounds by playing musical instruments. |
| | LANGUAGE, VERBALIZATION |
| LANOWN | For own sake; no explicit rationale offered for activity; encourage child to talk; using words to describe what one sees, thinks, feels; increasing vocabulary. |
| LANDR | Language drill, e.g., identity, "not" and yes-no statements; plurals; opposites; prepositions; correcting syntax; reciting days of week, months of year; analogies. |
| LANREL | To emphasize relations, e.g., classification with the words "same" and "different"; spatial relations with the words "over," "under," "on top of," etc.; temporal relations with the words "first," "next," "last"; if-then statements; talking about field trips and school routines sequentially; reviewing the activities done during that home visit in order; seriation with big and little, long and short, loud and soft sounds, etc.; following two to three verbal commands sequentially; verbalization in role play. |
| | OBJECT IDENTIFICATION (e.g., body parts, colors, letters, numbers, matching games like Lotto and Candyland) |
| OBOWN | For own sake; no explicit rationale offered for activity; to learn names of colors, letters, numbers, body parts, objects; naming parts of objects; to explore what objects look like and what they are made of. |
| OBUNIT | As part of unit, e.g., naming zoo and farm animals; naming community helpers from pictures. |
| OBACAD | To emphasize pre-academic skills, e.g., to discriminate own name from others; to discriminate various shapes from one another; identify letters with eyes closed; identify numbers; labelling and grouping objects in order to review language drill and identity, yes-no, opposite, and plural statements; naming body parts with identity statements; saying alphabet and identifying (pointing to) letters. |
| OBREL | To emphasize relations, e.g., to classify according to the "rule" for each category such as color, vehicleness, people vs. cars; to combine classifi- |

**Table 9**

*Variables for Description of Home Visit Activities (continued)*

| Variable | Description |
|---|---|
| | cation and seriation tasks such as big cars and little cars are all cars; spatial relationships of body parts to one another; recognizing missing parts; relational objects such as knife and fork; using objects appropriate to the role one is playing; classification by object characteristics such as shape, texture, smell, etc.; conservation tasks; object transformations such as adding yellow to blue playdoh to make green. |

READING

| Variable | Description |
|---|---|
| RDOWN | Teacher reads story for its own sake; no explicit rationale offered for activity; to listen to story. |
| RDUNIT | Teacher reads story related to unit, e.g., Christmas book or story about community helpers. |
| RDACAD | Pre-academic; teacher and child use DISTAR sheets for sound discriminations; use book to review language drill statements. |
| RDREL | Teacher reads story to emphasize relations, e.g., seriation with book about "big" and "little"; classification with book about animals; spatial relations with book about body parts; number books that emphasize a certain number of objects or counting the number of each kind of animal in an animal book. |

NUMBERS, ARITHMETIC

| Variable | Description |
|---|---|
| NOROTE | Rote counting. |
| NORULE | Counting in order to learn "rules"; identify statements for numbers; recognize and discriminate numbers such as with Number Bingo game; adding rules and subtracting rules; rules for telling time; algebraic equations such as $6 + \rule{1cm}{0.15mm} = 7$. |
| NOREL | To emphasize relations, e.g., seriation by counting objects, one-to-one correspondence; relationships like "more" and "less"; relative amounts of ingredients while making playdoh or cookies; playing with tea set by one-to-one correspondence of cups and saucers. |

FIELD TRIPS (teacher and child go someplace other than home visit site during the session)

| Variable | Description |
|---|---|
| TRUNIT | As part of unit, e.g., firehouse; museum for animals; walk outside for springtime unit; go to teacher's house to look at household items and appliances. |
| TRACAD | To emphasize specific preacademic skills, e.g., identity statements in department store; letter recognition at the supermarket. |
| TRREL | To emphasize relations, e.g., classification in department store; seriation of animals by size in pet store; temporal sequence in getting from a seed to a flower. |

SOCIAL-EMOTIONAL

| Variable | Description |
|---|---|
| SOCATT | Increasing attention span and control; decreasing impulsivity. |
| SOCMAN | Teaching correct manners, e.g., table manners; saying please and thank you. |
| SOCCO | Emphasizing cooperative play, sharing, taking turns; learning that one sometimes loses; working together on a task while making cookies; taking complementary roles. |
| SOCEGO | Explicitly stated goal of boosting child's self-confidence; increasing feelings of competence and self-worth; positive reinforcement of child either materially (e.g., M & M's) or verbally. |

### Table 10

#### Post-Hoc Comparisons of Group Activity Areas

| | Number of Agreements | | | |
| | Activity Done | Activity Not Done | Number of Disagreements | Percent of Agreement |
| Variable | | | | |
|---|---|---|---|---|
| **Visual-Motor** | | | | |
| VMOWN | 8 | 7 | 0 | 100.0 |
| VMUNIT | 3 | 12 | 0 | 100.0 |
| VMACAD | 5 | 10 | 0 | 100.0 |
| VMREL | 5 | 10 | 0 | 100.0 |
| **Language** | | | | |
| LANOWN | 6 | 8 | 1 | 93.3 |
| LANDR | 5 | 10 | 0 | 100.0 |
| LANREL | 5 | 9 | 1 | 93.3 |
| **Object Identification** | | | | |
| OBOWN | 4 | 9 | 2 | 86.7 |
| OBUNIT | 3 | 12 | 0 | 100.0 |
| OBACAD | 5 | 10 | 0 | 100.0 |
| OBREL | 7 | 7 | 1 | 93.3 |
| **Reading** | | | | |
| RDOWN | 3 | 11 | 1 | 93.3 |
| RDUNIT | 4 | 11 | 0 | 100.0 |
| RDACAD | 4 | 11 | 0 | 100.0 |
| RDREL | 3 | 11 | 1 | 93.3 |
| **Numbers** | | | | |
| NOROTE | 4 | 10 | 1 | 93.3 |
| NORULE | 5 | 10 | 0 | 100.0 |
| NOREL | 3 | 11 | 1 | 93.3 |
| **Field Trips** | | | | |
| TRUNIT | 2 | 13 | 0 | 100.0 |
| TRACAD | 1 | 14 | 0 | 100.0 |
| TRREL | 2 | 13 | 0 | 100.0 |
| **Social-Emotional** | | | | |
| SOCATT | 3 | 10 | 2 | 86.7 |
| SOCMAN | 1 | 14 | 0 | 100.0 |
| SOCCO | 3 | 11 | 1 | 93.3 |
| SOCEGO | 2 | 12 | 1 | 93.3 |

### Table 11

#### Home Visit Activity Areas: Comparison by Group

| | Cognitive (N=11) | | Language (N=15) | | Unit-Based (N=13) | | |
| Variable | Mean | S.D. | Mean | S.D. | Mean | S.D. | F Ratio |
|---|---|---|---|---|---|---|---|
| **Visual-Motor** | | | | | | | |
| (VM) | 5.05 | .14 | 5.16 | .13 | 5.09 | .16 | 2.00 |
| **Language** | | | | | | | |
| (LAN) | 4.02 | .05 | 3.99 | .02 | 3.95 | .07 | 4.95* |
| **Object Identification** | | | | | | | |
| (OB) | 3.99 | .07 | 3.98 | .03 | 3.58 | .09 | 157.84** |
| **Reading** | | | | | | | |
| (RD) | 4.36 | .13 | 4.90 | .09 | 4.77 | .21 | 42.80** |
| **Numbers** | | | | | | | |
| (NO) | 3.46 | .15 | 3.91 | .13 | 3.50 | .20 | 32.94* |
| **Field Trips** | | | | | | | |
| (TR) | 3.03 | .05 | 3.01 | .02 | 3.10 | .07 | 10.87** |
| **Social-Emotional** | | | | | | | |
| (SOC) | 4.44 | .25 | 4.04 | .04 | 4.56 | .17 | 37.76** |

*p<.05.
**p<.01.

**Table 12**

*Post-Hoc Comparisons of Group Activity Areas*

|                    | Cognitive                                                      | Language                                                    | Unit-Based                                                                                                      |
| ------------------ | -------------------------------------------------------------- | ---------------------------------------------------------- | -------------------------------------------------------------------------------------------------------------- |
| Compared with:     |                                                                |                                                            |                                                                                                                |
| Cognitive          |                                                                | LESS:<br>  Social-Emotional<br><br>MORE:<br>  Reading<br>  Numbers | LESS:<br>  Language<br>  Object Identification<br><br>MORE:<br>  Reading<br>  Field Trips                        |
| Language           | LESS:<br>  Reading<br>  Numbers<br><br>MORE:<br>  Social-Emotional | | LESS:<br>  Language<br>  Object Identification<br>  Reading<br>  Numbers<br><br>MORE:<br>  Field Trips<br>  Social-Emotional |
| Unit-Based         | LESS:<br>  Reading<br>  Field Trips<br><br>MORE:<br>  Language<br>  Object Identification | LESS:<br>  Field Trips<br>  Social-Emotional<br><br>MORE:<br>  Language<br>  Object Identification<br>  Reading<br>  Numbers | |

NOTE: Differences listed are significant at $p < .05$.

than the other two programs, and less emphasis on social-emotional concerns. Finally, the Unit-Based Program offered the fewest language and object-identification activities and the most field trips and social-emotional activities during home visits.

These results are consistent with curriculum models. The Language Program was designed to emphasize pre-academic skills, hence the children were involved in reading and number activities more than children in the other two groups. Social-emotional activities were tangential to the major concerns of the Language Program and received little attention during home visits. Unit-Based teachers did not have either a well defined basis or a method for presenting language and object-identification activities when compared to Language and Cognitive teachers; it is therefore understandable that these areas were stressed least in the Unit-Based group. Instead, Unit-Based teachers promoted social-emotional development, an area which receives emphasis in traditional preschool models, and took the children on field trips to unit-related community sites. It should be noted, however, that field trips had a low frequency of occurrence in all three curricula, perhaps because they were more appropriate to the large-group classroom setting than to the individualized home visits. Significant program differences on this variable may be largely attributable to the small within-group variance. Finally, the finding that children in the Cognitive Program had the fewest reading activities reflects differences between that program and each of the other two. In relation to the Language Program, where children actually read from worksheets, the Cognitive Program of course did not stress this academic skill. In comparison with the Unit-Based Program, it can be said that

Cognitive Program children were less often read *to* by their teachers. One is relatively passive when being read to, and the emphasis in the Cognitive Program was on learning and structuring one's thoughts by "doing."

Table 13 presents the results of one-way analyses of variance comparing groups for each of the 25 home visit activity variables. Significant program differences were found for all variables, due in large part to small within-program variances rather than to large differences in means. Post-hoc comparisons of the three groups, summarized in table 14, were consistent with expectations based on curriculum descriptions. Specifically, activities done during the Cognitive Program home visits emphasized spatial and temporal relations, classification, seriation, and so forth, significantly more than the other two programs, which did not differ from each other. Activities done during Language home visits

**Table 13**

*Home Visit Activities: Comparison by Group*

| | Cognitive (N=11) | | Language (N=15) | | Unit-Based (N=13) | | |
|---|---|---|---|---|---|---|---|
| | Mean | S.D. | Mean | S.D. | Mean | S.D. | F Ratio |
| **Visual-Motor** | | | | | | | |
| VMOWN | 1.16 | .09 | 1.29 | .15 | 1.62 | .15 | 37.0** |
| VMUNIT | 1.00 | .02 | 1.00 | .01 | 1.47 | .07 | 547.0** |
| VMACAD | 1.00 | .00 | 1.87 | .09 | 1.00 | .00 | 1025.9** |
| VMREL | 1.89 | .09 | 1.00 | .00 | 1.01 | .02 | 1434.8** |
| **Language** | | | | | | | |
| LANOWN | 1.03 | .05 | 1.00 | .00 | 1.94 | .06 | 1926.2** |
| LANDR | 1.01 | .02 | 1.99 | .02 | 1.01 | .02 | 13206.0** |
| LANREL | 1.98 | .04 | 1.00 | .00 | 1.00 | .01 | 6387.2** |
| **Object Identification** | | | | | | | |
| OBOWN | 1.01 | .03 | 1.00 | .01 | 1.57 | .22 | 84.6** |
| OBUNIT | 1.00 | .01 | 1.01 | .02 | 1.57 | .11 | 331.5** |
| OBACAD | 1.02 | .04 | 1.98 | .04 | 1.00 | .00 | 4147.0** |
| OBREL | 1.97 | .03 | 1.00 | .01 | 1.01 | .04 | 4535.0** |
| **Reading** | | | | | | | |
| RDOWN | 1.00 | .00 | 1.05 | .04 | 1.20 | .09 | 39.7** |
| RDUNIT | 1.00 | .00 | 1.01 | .03 | 1.56 | .16 | 147.3** |
| RDACAD | 1.00 | .00 | 1.83 | .09 | 1.00 | .00 | 1020.8** |
| RDREL | 1.36 | .13 | 1.00 | .00 | 1.01 | .02 | 110.2** |
| **Numbers** | | | | | | | |
| NOROTE | 1.01 | .02 | 1.09 | .07 | 1.43 | .13 | 76.2** |
| NORULE | 1.00 | .00 | 1.79 | .10 | 1.00 | .01 | 680.4** |
| NOREL | 1.46 | .14 | 1.03 | .05 | 1.07 | .08 | 77.5** |
| **Field Trips** | | | | | | | |
| TRUNIT | 1.00 | .00 | 1.00 | .00 | 1.10 | .07 | 25.7** |
| TRACAD | 1.00 | .00 | 1.01 | .02 | 1.00 | .00 | 4.0* |
| TRREL | 1.03 | .05 | 1.00 | .00 | 1.00 | .00 | 4.5* |
| **Social-Emotional** | | | | | | | |
| SOCATT | 1.15 | .15 | 1.01 | .02 | 1.23 | .12 | 16.3** |
| SOCMAN | 1.00 | .00 | 1.00 | .00 | 1.01 | .02 | 3.5* |
| SOCCO | 1.16 | .12 | 1.01 | .03 | 1.22 | .13 | 16.3** |
| SOCEGO | 1.12 | .09 | 1.02 | .03 | 1.10 | .07 | 9.5** |

*$p<.05$.
**$p<.01$.

**Table 14**

*Post-Hoc Comparisons by Group of Home Visit Activities*

| C>L, U | L>C, U | U>C, L |
|---|---|---|
| Visual-Motor: Relations | Visual-Motor: Academic | Visual-Motor: Own Sake |
| Language: Relations | Object Identification: Academic | Language: Own Sake |
| Object Identification: Relations | Reading: Academic | Object Identification: Own Sake |
| Reading: Relations | Trips: Academic | Reading: Own Sake |
| Numbers: Relations | Language: Drill | Visual-Motor: Unit Themes |
| Trips: Relations | Numbers: Rules | Object Identification: Unit Themes |
| Social-emotional: Self-confidence | | Reading: Unit Themes |
| | | Trips: Unit Themes |
| | | Numbers: Rote |
| | | Social-emotional: Attention Span |
| | | Social-emotional: Manners |
| | | Social-emotional: Cooperation |

| C>L | | U>L |
|---|---|---|
| Social-emotional: Attention Span | | Social-emotional: Self-confidence |
| Social-emotional: Cooperation | | |

stressed academic skills, numerical rules, and language drill to a greater extent than the other two programs, which were not significantly different from one another. In the Unit-Based Program, activities were more often done for their own sake (i.e., without explicit rationales offered) or to emphasize the themes in a unit than was the case in either the Cognitive or the Language program. Finally, as was seen before, social-emotional variables were emphasized most in the Unit-Based Program and least in the Language Program.

Tables 15-17 present the results of three one-way analyses of variance comparing teachers or teacher pairs on the home visit activity variables within the Cognitive, Language, and Unit-Based programs, respectively.[18]

---

[18]Four one-way analyses of variance (one for Group, three for Teacher-within-Group) were computed for each variable, rather than a two-way (Group-by-Teacher) analysis of variance because of the completely nested design. It is acknowledged that the variance in the three Teacher-within-Group ANOVAs is actually a partition of the same variance found in the Group ANOVA. Because there is no acceptable way to adjust the degrees of freedom in this case, the reader might want to interpret the probability levels of the Teacher-within-Group F ratios conservatively (e.g., use $p<.01$ rather than $p<.05$ to establish significance).

**Table 15**

*Home Visit Acitivites: Teachers Within the Cognitive Program*

| | Teacher or Teacher Pair | | | | | | | | |
| | 1 (N=3) | | 2 (N=4) | | 3 (N=2) | | 4 (N=2) | | |
| Variable | Mean | S.D. | Mean | S.D. | Mean | S.D. | Mean | S.D. | F Ratio |
|---|---|---|---|---|---|---|---|---|---|
| VMOWN | 1.19 | .09 | 1.21 | .09 | 1.13 | .00 | 1.05 | .07 | 1.81 |
| VMUNIT | 1.00 | .00 | 1.00 | .00 | 1.00 | .00 | 1.03 | .04 | 1.91 |
| VMACAD | 1.00 | .00 | 1.00 | .00 | 1.00 | .00 | 1.00 | .00 | (a) |
| VMREL | 1.90 | .06 | 1.92 | .07 | 1.83 | .18 | 1.84 | .07 | 0.60 |
| LANOWN | 1.03 | .02 | 1.00 | .00 | 1.13 | .00 | 1.00 | .00 | 45.23** |
| LANDR | 1.00 | .00 | 1.00 | .00 | 1.04 | .00 | 1.00 | .00 | (a) |
| LANREL | 1.96 | .04 | 2.00 | .00 | 1.94 | .09 | 2.00 | .00 | 1.51 |
| OBOWN | 1.00 | .00 | 1.00 | .00 | 1.06 | .03 | 1.00 | .00 | 17.18** |
| OBUNIT | 1.00 | .00 | 1.00 | .00 | 1.02 | .03 | 1.00 | .01 | 1.91 |
| OBACAD | 1.02 | .03 | 1.00 | .00 | 1.06 | .09 | 1.00 | .00 | 1.39 |
| OBREL | 1.94 | .02 | 1.99 | .03 | 1.98 | .03 | 1.97 | .04 | 1.89 |
| RDOWN | 1.00 | .00 | 1.00 | .00 | 1.00 | .00 | 1.00 | .00 | (a) |
| RDUNIT | 1.00 | .00 | 1.00 | .00 | 1.00 | .00 | 1.00 | .00 | (a) |
| RDACAD | 1.00 | .00 | 1.00 | .00 | 1.00 | .00 | 1.00 | .00 | (a) |
| RDREL | 1.25 | .04 | 1.45 | .10 | 1.35 | .15 | 1.34 | .19 | 1.78 |
| NOROTE | 1.01 | .02 | 1.00 | .00 | 1.00 | .00 | 1.03 | .04 | 1.06 |
| NORULE | 1.00 | .00 | 1.00 | .00 | 1.00 | .00 | 1.00 | .00 | (a) |
| NOREL | 1.48 | .08 | 1.55 | .07 | 1.29 | .06 | 1.39 | .26 | 2.41 |
| TRUNIT | 1.00 | .00 | 1.00 | .00 | 1.00 | .00 | 1.00 | .00 | (a) |
| TRACAD | 1.00 | .00 | 1.00 | .00 | 1.00 | .00 | 1.00 | .00 | (a) |
| TRREL | 1.03 | .03 | 1.01 | .03 | 1.08 | .12 | 1.00 | .00 | 1.14 |
| SOCATT | 1.03 | .03 | 1.18 | .02 | 1.21 | .18 | 1.24 | .33 | 1.04 |
| SOCMAN | 1.00 | .00 | 1.00 | .00 | 1.00 | .00 | 1.00 | .00 | (a) |
| SOCCO | 1.09 | .07 | 1.19 | .12 | 1.23 | .09 | 1.13 | .19 | 0.76 |
| SOCEGO | 1.14 | .05 | 1.11 | .07 | 1.17 | .18 | 1.08 | .11 | 0.35 |

(a)—Unable to compute F ratio because variance = 0.

**p<.01.

Most F ratios were nonsignificant, indicating that children in the same program did *not* receive different teaching experiences on those variables, even though they had a different teacher (or pair of teachers) making home visits. A few variables did show a significant Teacher-within-Group effect, and again even these may be attributable to the small within-teacher (or within-teacher pair) variances. In the Cognitive Program, two activities showed a significant teacher difference—language and object identification for their own sake. This may merely reflect the neglect of some teacher(s) to specify the rationale for these two activities in their home visit reports. In the Language Program, there were also only two activities with a significant teacher effect—reading to stress a unit and numerical relations. The first difference may reflect one teacher's traditional training; the second may reflect previous training in using one-to-one correspondence in learning numbers or the concurrent influence of the cognitive approach.

In all cases of significant teacher differences in the Cognitive and Language programs, however, the differences in mean frequencies were quite small and achieved significance by virtue of small within-teacher

**Table 16**

*Home Visit Activities: Teachers Within the Language Program*

| | Teacher or Teacher Pair | | | | | | | | | | | | | |
| --- | --- | --- | --- | --- | --- | --- | --- | --- | --- | --- | --- | --- | --- | --- |
| | 1 (N=1) | | 2 (N=3) | | 3 (N=1) | | 4 (N=2) | | 5 (N=5) | | 6 (N=1) | | 7 (N=2) | | F Ratio |
| Variable | Mean | S.D. | Mean | S.D. | Mean | S.D. | Mean | S.D. | Mean | S.D. | Mean | S.D. | Mean | S.D. | |
| VMOWN | 1.38 | .00 | 1.26 | .09 | 1.63 | .00 | 1.37 | .09 | 1.21 | .15 | 1.21 | .00 | 1.27 | .16 | 1.63 |
| VMUNIT | 1.00 | .00 | 1.00 | .00 | 1.00 | .00 | 1.00 | .00 | 1.01 | .03 | 1.00 | .00 | 1.00 | .00 | 0.22 |
| VMACAD | 1.75 | .00 | 1.89 | .09 | 1.75 | .00 | 1.91 | .01 | 1.89 | .06 | 1.95 | .00 | 1.81 | .20 | 0.93 |
| VMREL | 1.00 | .00 | 1.00 | .00 | 1.00 | .00 | 1.00 | .00 | 1.00 | .00 | 1.00 | .00 | 1.00 | .00 | (a) |
| LANOWN | 1.00 | .00 | 1.00 | .00 | 1.00 | .00 | 1.00 | .00 | 1.00 | .00 | 1.00 | .00 | 1.00 | .00 | (a) |
| LANDR | 1.96 | .00 | 2.00 | .00 | 2.00 | .00 | 2.00 | .00 | 1.98 | .03 | 2.00 | .00 | 2.00 | .00 | 0.98 |
| LANREL | 1.00 | .00 | 1.00 | .00 | 1.00 | .00 | 1.00 | .00 | 1.00 | .00 | 1.00 | .00 | 1.00 | .00 | (a) |
| OBOWN | 1.00 | .00 | 1.02 | .03 | 1.00 | .00 | 1.00 | .00 | 1.00 | .00 | 1.00 | .00 | 1.00 | .00 | 0.53 |
| OBUNIT | 1.00 | .00 | 1.02 | .03 | 1.04 | .00 | 1.00 | .00 | 1.00 | .00 | 1.00 | .00 | 1.00 | .00 | 1.49 |
| OBACAD | 2.00 | .00 | 1.96 | .06 | 2.00 | .00 | 2.00 | .00 | 1.98 | .03 | 2.00 | .00 | 1.92 | .04 | 1.06 |
| OBREL | 1.00 | .00 | 1.00 | .00 | 1.00 | .00 | 1.00 | .00 | 1.00 | .00 | 1.00 | .00 | 1.03 | .04 | 1.56 |
| RDOWN | 1.04 | .00 | 1.07 | .03 | 1.00 | .00 | 1.07 | .04 | 1.05 | .05 | 1.00 | .00 | 1.05 | .00 | 0.64 |
| RDUNIT | 1.00 | .00 | 1.00 | .00 | 1.00 | .00 | 1.00 | .00 | 1.01 | .02 | 1.11 | .00 | 1.00 | .00 | 5.39* |
| RDACAD | 1.71 | .00 | 1.84 | .05 | 1.83 | .00 | 1.84 | .04 | 1.79 | .11 | 1.89 | .00 | 1.95 | .07 | 1.21 |
| RDREL | 1.00 | .00 | 1.00 | .00 | 1.00 | .00 | 1.00 | .00 | 1.00 | .00 | 1.00 | .00 | 1.00 | .00 | (a) |
| NOROTE | 1.21 | .00 | 1.11 | .09 | 1.08 | .00 | 1.02 | .03 | 1.08 | .08 | 1.16 | .00 | 1.08 | .04 | 0.84 |
| NORULE | 1.71 | .00 | 1.77 | .06 | 1.88 | .00 | 1.89 | .02 | 1.75 | .09 | 1.79 | .00 | 1.82 | .26 | 0.53 |
| NOREL | 1.00 | .00 | 1.02 | .03 | 1.08 | .00 | 1.11 | .04 | 1.00 | .00 | 1.00 | .00 | 1.03 | .04 | 6.67** |
| TRUNIT | 1.00 | .00 | 1.00 | .00 | 1.00 | .00 | 1.00 | .00 | 1.00 | .00 | 1.00 | .00 | 1.00 | .00 | (a) |
| TRACAD | 1.00 | .00 | 1.02 | .03 | 1.00 | .00 | 1.00 | .00 | 1.03 | .03 | 1.00 | .00 | 1.00 | .00 | 0.77 |
| TRREL | 1.00 | .00 | 1.00 | .00 | 1.00 | .00 | 1.00 | .00 | 1.00 | .00 | 1.00 | .00 | 1.00 | .00 | (a) |
| SOCATT | 1.00 | .00 | 1.00 | .00 | 1.00 | .00 | 1.00 | .00 | 1.01 | .03 | 1.00 | .00 | 1.03 | .04 | 0.42 |
| SOCMAN | 1.00 | .00 | 1.00 | .00 | 1.00 | .00 | 1.00 | .00 | 1.00 | .00 | 1.00 | .00 | 1.00 | .00 | (a) |
| SOCCO | 1.00 | .00 | 1.04 | .06 | 1.00 | .00 | 1.00 | .00 | 1.02 | .03 | 1.00 | .00 | 1.00 | .00 | 0.37 |
| SOCEGO | 1.04 | .00 | 1.05 | .05 | 1.00 | .00 | 1.02 | .03 | 1.00 | .00 | 1.00 | .00 | 1.00 | .00 | 1.42 |

(a)—Unable to compute F ratio because variance = 0.

*p<.05.

**p<.01

**Table 17**

Home Visit Activities: Teachers Within the Unit-Based Program

| | Teacher | | | | |
|---|---|---|---|---|---|
| | 1 (N=7) | | 2 (N=6) | | |
| Variable | Mean | S.D. | Mean | S.D. | F Ratio |
| VMOWN | 1.51 | .08 | 1.74 | .12 | 17.14** |
| VMUNIT | 1.48 | .07 | 1.45 | .06 | 0.60 |
| VMACAD | 1.00 | .00 | 1.00 | .00 | (a) |
| VMREL | 1.00 | .00 | 1.02 | .02 | 2.96 |
| LANOWN | 1.91 | .06 | 1.98 | .03 | 6.74* |
| LANDR | 1.00 | .00 | 1.01 | .02 | 2.95 |
| LANREL | 1.00 | .00 | 1.07 | .02 | 1.18 |
| OBOWN | 1.40 | .07 | 1.78 | .12 | 58.37** |
| OBUNIT | 1.61 | .08 | 1.53 | .13 | 1.90 |
| OBACAD | 1.00 | .00 | 1.00 | .00 | (a) |
| OBREL | 1.00 | .00 | 1.02 | .06 | 1.18 |
| RDOWN | 1.17 | .08 | 1.24 | .09 | 2.36 |
| RDUNIT | 1.46 | .10 | 1.68 | .14 | 10.76** |
| RDACAD | 1.00 | .00 | 1.00 | .00 | (a) |
| RDREL | 1.01 | .02 | 1.01 | .02 | 0.04 |
| NOROTE | 1.35 | .11 | 1.52 | .08 | 9.77** |
| NORULE | 1.00 | .00 | 1.01 | .02 | 1.18 |
| NOREL | 1.03 | .04 | 1.12 | .10 | 4.71 |
| TRUNIT | 1.14 | .07 | 1.06 | .05 | 5.92* |
| TRACAD | 1.00 | .00 | 1.00 | .00 | (a) |
| TRREL | 1.00 | .00 | 1.00 | .00 | (a) |
| SOCATT | 1.26 | .13 | 1.20 | .11 | 0.85 |
| SOCMAN | 1.01 | .03 | 1.01 | .02 | 0.34 |
| SOCCO | 1.17 | .10 | 1.29 | .14 | 3.22 |
| SOCEGO | 1.13 | .08 | 1.06 | .05 | 3.57 |

(a)—Unable to compute F ratio because variance = 0.

*$p < .05$.
**$p < .01$.

variances. More activity differences emerged between the two teachers in the Unit-Based Program. Of six significant differences, four involved doing activities for their own sake, and these may again reflect differences in individual styles in explicitly noting rationales in written reports. The other two differences showed one teacher taking unit-related field trips slightly more often than the second, and the second teacher reading unit-related books more frequently than the first. This may merely reflect a difference in individual preference for the kind of activity used to focus on a unit. In no case, however, was a teacher activity difference within the Unit-Based Program counterbalanced by one or both teachers doing activities appropriate to one of the other two programs.

The greater number of significant teacher differences in the Unit-Based Program compared to the Cognitive and Language programs may reflect the differential clarity of the three curriculum models. The Cognitive and Language programs provided clearly defined theories and methodologies; the Unit-Based Program provided neither. As a result, the Cognitive and Language teachers may have had more explicit directions about the "why" as well as the "what" of activities. Teachers in the

Unit-Based Program operated with less well defined, more personal rationales and hence had room to vary more within the curriculum guidelines.

Despite some teacher differences in all three programs, it can be concluded that program differences exceeded teacher differences. Programs were significantly different from one another on all 25 home visit activity variables; teachers within programs were significantly different from one another on only a few variables. Furthermore, each program as a whole, as well as each teacher or teacher pair within each program, engaged the child in home visit activities which were consistent with curriculum models.

## Summary of the three programs as reflected in the HVRs

Home Visit Reports were analyzed to examine program differences in three areas: the setting, maternal behavior, and curriculum operation.

Home visits in the Cognitive Program were characterized by a high degree of maternal participation. There was some evidence that mothers increased their feedback requests and expansiveness in their informational exchanges with their children over the two-year period. The activities which teachers did with children in the home emphasized active participation and covered such areas as spatial and temporal relations, classification, and seriation. Teachers engaged the children in home visit activities which were consistent with activities of the other Cognitive Program teachers as well as with the stated objectives of the Cognitive Curriculum.

In the Language Program, mothers also participated a great deal in the home teaching sessions. Activities stressed academic skills such as number and letter recognition, numerical rules for simple arithmetic operations, and language drill. Areas of social-emotional development were emphasized less than they were in the other two programs. As in the Cognitive Program, teachers in the Language Program were consistent with one another in their home visit activities as well as in following the explicit model of the Language Curriculum.

Maternal participation in the Unit-Based Program was not as great as in the Cognitive and Language programs. Mothers in the Unit-Based Program were involved in an average of only 50% of the home teaching sessions, compared with 80% for mothers in the other two groups. This lower level of maternal involvement could be attributed to a less clearly defined role for mothers in Unit-Based home activities. Teachers spent less time in language and object-identification activities, perhaps because the curriculum had a less explicit basis and method for presenting these activities than did the other two curricula. Children were either engaged in activities for their own sake or else worked with art materials, motor games, objects, books, and songs related to the themes of a unit. The Unit-Based Program included social-emotional goals in home visit activities to a greater degree than did the Cognitive or the Language program. Finally, although Unit-Based teachers differed somewhat more from one another in activities done than did teachers in the other two programs, they still maintained consistency within a broadly defined traditional preschool model which accommodates the creativity of the individual teacher and, more specifically, within a curriculum centered around unit themes for learning.

Analyses of the Home Visit Reports support the contention that this is a "curriculum demonstration" study. Despite some differences in maternal involvement, the setting (e.g., length of visit, readiness of mother and child, participation by other children, use of materials between visits, maternal questions about the curriculum) was basically the same for all three curricula. This consistency of program operation becomes a background against which differences attributable to curriculum models can be examined. A comparison of home visit activities for each of the three programs demonstrates that there were indeed three distinct curricula operating. Programs were distinguished from one another in both the areas of activity which they stressed and the rationale behind their differential emphases. Teachers in the Cognitive Program stressed cognitive relations; teachers in the Language Program stressed language and pre-academic skills; and teachers in the Unit-Based Program stressed the themes of the current classroom unit. In short, the home visit activities operationalized three distinct curriculum models. Further, examination of the Home Visit Reports substantiates the crucial contention that the variance in content found between these three programs exceeds the variance found between teachers or pairs of teachers within the same program. Thus, the CD Project does compare programs, not teachers.

# VERIFICATION OF PROGRAM OPERATION: A SUMMARY

The purpose of this chapter has been to document the operation of the Cognitive, Language, and Unit-Based programs with observations made in the classrooms and in children's homes. Both systematic and subjective observational techniques were used in this documentation process. Systematic classroom observations were made by trained observers using the categories of the Pupil Record of School Experiences (PROSE). Twelve consultants, specialists in areas related to early childhood education and development, visited the CD Project and recorded their observations of the three classrooms. In addition, objective analyses were performed on the teachers' descriptions of activities in their Home Visit Reports. Two major findings emerged from these three sources of observation:

- The differences between the three programs in terms of content and processes were greater than the differences between teachers within the same program. This justifies the claim that the CD Project compares curricula rather than teachers.
- The activities and processes observed in each of the three programs were consistent with the models on which they were based. In other words, three distinct curricula were being implemented in both the classroom and the home.

Observations pointed to certain commonalities which, by design, were shared by the three preschool programs. Within all classrooms, staff enthusiasm and commitment were high. All three curricula emphasized the development of language skills and task persistence, although the programs differed in their methods and the extent to which these areas were emphasized. Within the home, such setting variables as length of visit, preparation of family, and presence of mother were comparable across the three programs.

The Language Program was seen to be highly structured with adults directing groups of children in academic tasks. Positive reinforcement was used extensively by teachers. The clear division between work and nonwork time resulted in little spontaneous social interaction between teachers and children and among the children themselves. In the home, mothers participated together with teachers in engaging children in academically oriented activities.

In the Cognitive Program, teachers showed the greatest amount of attention to the individual child by supporting learning at the child's level of cognitive development rather than by using direct teaching techniques. Maternal involvement in the home visits was high, and teachers concentrated on such Piagetian concepts as seriation and classification when working with the family.

The Unit-Based Program was observed to be the least structured of the three classrooms, with children consequently showing much individual variation in task persistence and sustained attention. Children in this curriculum exhibited the greatest amount of divergent activity and expressions of fantasy, as well as the highest levels of spontaneous social interaction with teachers and peers. Maternal participation in the home visits was lower than in the other two programs, and teachers stressed unit themes and social-emotional goals during home sessions.

Having established these program distinctions, we proceed in the next chapter to address the question of differential program impact in two related areas: teachers' perceptions of children's classroom behavior, and the parent-child relationship and parents' attitudes toward education.

# IV Child ratings by teachers and parents

Children in the CD Project were rated by their preschool teachers at the end of the program and by their elementary school teachers in the spring of first and second grade. In addition, CD Project parents were interviewed when the children were in fourth grade and ratings were derived from parents' responses to questions about their relationship with their children.

Four rating instruments were used by teachers and parents. Preschool teachers used two instruments to rate children at the end of preschool: the Pupil Observation Checklist (POCL) and the Classroom Behavior Checklist, Version 1 (CBCL-1). Elementary school teachers used the Classroom Behavior Checklist, Version 2 (CBCL-2) to rate children in the spring of grades 1 and 2. The Parent Interview, focusing on various aspects of the family and parent-child relationships, was administered during the spring of the children's fourth-grade year.

This chapter presents descriptions of the instruments used and the results of the child ratings by teachers and parents. The chapter is organized as follows:

- Ratings by Preschool Teachers
- Ratings by Elementary School Teachers
- Relationship Between Teacher Ratings and Nonprogram Variables
- Ratings by Parents
- Summary of Ratings by Teachers and Parents

# RATINGS BY PRESCHOOL TEACHERS

## Development of instruments

**The POCL.**   The POCL, a set of 25 7-point rating scales, was developed in 1968 by David Weikart in consultation with CD Project teachers and supervisors. The 25 scales were defined by pairs of adjectives or adjective phrases, as listed in table 18. The table lists the positive descriptor first, although the order of positive and negative descriptors was varied on the actual instrument.

The list is also ordered according to the results of a factor analysis. Although the CD Project had too small a sample for a factor analysis, the POCL was also used by elementary school teachers at High/Scope Foundation sites in the national Follow Through project. Despite the possibility of differences between preschool teachers and Follow Through teachers, the grouping of POCL items into factors makes the results of its administration more valid and interpretable. In the Follow Through project, two teachers at each of three sites using the Cognitive Curriculum made POCL ratings. These six teachers rated primary grade children in the fall of 1968 and again in the spring of 1969, resulting in a total of 1185 ratings. Subsamples of these ratings were entered into a principal-components factor analysis, followed by varimax rotation. The same factors appeared at fall and at spring and within each site.[19] Inspection of the factor loadings suggested that the factors be named sociability, cooperation, and academic orientation. The items with significant factor loadings appear in table 18 under the appropriate factor labels. A child's rating for a given factor was the mean rating of the items listed for that factor. This rating shall be called a factor rating, to distinguish it from factor scores which are calculated in other ways. The remaining nine items, which did not load significantly on any factor, were excluded from further analysis.[20]

The reliability of CD Project raters using the POCL may be estimated if certain assumptions are accepted. Although children and teacher/raters were nested within programs and waves, two preschool teachers rated each child. By combining ratings across programs and across waves, a sample of 41 children was obtained, each child being rated by a pair of teachers. The product-moment correlations between the factor ratings of one teacher and the other teacher in all pairs provided an estimate of inter-rater reliability. The correlations were as follows: sociability, .65; cooperation, .63; academic orientation, .70. While these correlations would be somewhat low for trained raters, they are surprisingly good for teachers who had not received extensive training in the use of the instrument. They certainly permit further exploration of the variables.

**The CBCL-1.**    The other instrument used by preschool teachers was the CBCL-1. The CBCL-1 was a set of 21 7-point rating scales developed in 1969 by Martin Heilweil of the CD Project staff. The scales were defined by the behavior descriptions that are listed in table 19. The CBCL-1 items were drawn from the Pupil Behavior Inventory (Vinter, Sarri, Vorwaller, & Schafer, 1966), other rating instruments, and teacher suggestions. The CBCL-1 differs from most rating instruments in that teachers were instructed to rate all children on one item at a time. This technique ought to prompt comparisons across children and reduce the tendency to rate items the same way for a given child.

As with the POCL, the CBCL-1 was used at the High/Scope Foundation's Follow Through sites and the results were factor-analyzed. A total of 10 teachers rated 134 children. The factors which emerged bore a strong resemblance to the factors of the POCL and were given the same names. Table 19 presents the factor loadings of CBCL-1 items.

The CBCL-1 was used in the CD Project in the same fashion as the POCL—children and teacher/raters nested within programs and waves. Again, inter-rater reliability was estimated by combining programs and waves and correlating factor ratings between pairs of teachers. The correlations were as follows: sociability, .69; cooperation, .68; academic orientation, .57. These correlations are similar in magnitude to the corresponding correlations for the POCL. Again, they permit further exploration of the variables.

---

[19]The POCL was also used by testers to rate children's behavior during test sessions. However, factors did not appear with consistency for testers in the Follow Through project, and the reliability of tester/raters was not assessed. For these reasons, tester ratings with the POCL were not further analyzed.

[20]Some of these remaining items (e.g., neatly dressed/poorly dressed) had been used to assess teacher bias. The fact that such items did not load on any factor indicates that teachers were not influenced by these dimensions.

**Table 18**

*Factor Structure of the POCL*

| Factor<br>Item | Factor<br>Loading |
|---|---|
| **Sociability** | |
| talkative/quiet | .95 |
| outgoing/withdrawn | .93 |
| sociable/shy | .90 |
| active/passive | .85 |
| **Cooperation** | |
| agreeable/defensive | .82 |
| imposing/compromising | .77 |
| cheerful/irritable | .75 |
| cooperative/resistive | .72 |
| **Academic Orientation** | |
| challenged by hard tasks/prefers easy tasks | .92 |
| persistent/gives up | .91 |
| attentive/inattentive | .82 |
| eager to continue/seeks to terminate | .82 |
| diligent/distracted | .80 |
| works independently/needs encouragement | .79 |
| good academic potential/poor academic potential | .75 |
| involved/indifferent | .70 |
| (Remaining Items) | |
| content/anxious | |
| eager/reluctant | |
| original/parroting | |
| complex language/limited language | |
| trusting/hesitant | |
| reflective/impulsive | |
| impressed by child/unimpressed by child | |
| neatly dressed/poorly dressed | |
| good hygiene/poor hygiene | |

**Table 19**

*Factor Structure of the CBCL-1*

| Factor<br>Item | Factor<br>Loading |
|---|---|
| **Sociability** | |
| Talks at free time | .88 |
| Initiates friendship | .86 |
| Has a sense of humor | .75 |
| Participates in group discussion | .74 |
| Talks easily about feelings | .68 |
| **Cooperation** | |
| Disrupts[1] | .87 |
| Attempts to manipulate teacher[1] | .87 |
| Obeys | .84 |
| Resents criticism or discipline[1] | .81 |
| **Academic Orientation** | |
| Motivated to academic performance | .79 |
| Acts with initiative in school work | .74 |
| Forgets learning quickly[1] | .74 |
| Makes new use of materials | .71 |
| Looks for artistic combinations of materials | .66 |
| (Remaining Items) | |
| Well received by other children | |
| Hesitates to try, gives up easily[1] | |
| Explores new objects | |
| Poor personal hygiene[1] | |
| Difficult to like[1] | |
| Answers when called on | |
| Seeks constant reassurance[1] | |

[1]Scale reversed because the descriptor is negative.

The similarity of factors on the POCL and the CBCL-1 is readily apparent. The validity of the factors would be supported by high correlations between ratings on the corresponding factors. The product-moment correlations between POCL factors and CBCL-1 factors of the same name were as follows: sociability, .89; cooperation, .61; academic orientation, .83. With a sample size of 43, all these correlations are highly significant. It appears, then, that the POCL and the CBCL-1 measured the same factors.

## Use of instruments

The POCL and CBCL-1 were used by CD Project preschool teachers to rate the classroom behavior of children as they completed preschool. Although ratings by a child's own teacher lack the objectivity of ratings by a trained and impartial observer, teachers were asked to complete the instruments because they were in a unique position to draw on accumulated knowledge of the children to inform their ratings.

Teachers thus rated children within the context of their particular program, i.e., children were compared with others in the same curriculum rather than across curricula or according to some "universal" standard. This procedure does not allow comparisons between programs on the factor ratings since program variance cannot be distinguished from rater variance. However, since the rating instruments were designed to distribute project children as a whole along each scale, the factor ratings of the children can be related to selected nonprogram variables. These relationships of factor ratings to demographic data collected in preschool and to achievement data collected during elementary school are explored in a later section of this chapter.

# RATINGS BY ELEMENTARY SCHOOL TEACHERS

## Development of instrument

The CBCL-2 was the successor of the CBCL-1. The CBCL-2 was a set of 15 7-point scales developed in 1969 and 1970 by Martin Heilweil of the CD Project staff. Table 20 presents the behavior descriptors which defined the scales. Teachers using this instrument returned to rating one child at a time on all items, but they were instructed to compare each child to all others in the class.

As with other rating instruments in the CD Project, a factor analysis of the CBCL-2 was "borrowed" from evaluations of High/Scope's Follow Through sites. A total of 58 teachers rated 400 children. The factors were similar to those found with the other instruments: sociability, cooperation, and academic orientation; plus an additional factor labeled independence. Table 20 reports the factor loadings of the CBCL-2 items.

## Use of instrument

Elementary school teachers, who had neither direct involvement nor extensive knowledge of the CD Project, were asked to rate children in

**Table 20**

*Factor Structure of the CBCL-2*

| Factor<br>Item | Factor<br>Loading |
|---|---|
| Sociability | |
| Talks at free time | .84 |
| Initiates friendships with others | .74 |
| Has a sense of humor | .71 |
| Cooperation | |
| Easy to get along with | .84 |
| Accepts criticism or discipline without resentment | .81 |
| Obeys | .79 |
| Academic Orientation | |
| Extends learning to new situations | .89 |
| Grasps concepts readily | .88 |
| Motivated to academic performance | .88 |
| Carries through a series of events | .86 |
| Independence | |
| Possessive of teacher[1] | .84 |
| Seeks constant reassurance[1] | .78 |
| (Remaining Items) | |
| Disrupts others[1] | |
| Enters into role play | |
| Participates in group discussion | |

[1]Scale reversed because the descriptor is negative.

their classrooms[21] who had participated in the three preschool programs. These ratings were filled out in the spring of both first and second grade. Teachers were paid two dollars for every rating form they returned.

The rate of return on Waves 6 and 7 at first grade was 29 of 41 or 71%; at second grade it was 28 of 41 or 68%. However, only 18 of the CD Project children were rated by teachers at both first and second grade. Although limited, this overlap does permit some estimate of the reliability of the CBCL-2 ratings. The correlations between the two sets of ratings were, of course, affected by two confounded sources of error: disagreement between teachers and longitudinal instability of the behaviors rated. The product-moment correlations between ratings by grade 1 teachers and ratings by grade 2 teachers were: sociability, .69; cooperation, .68; academic orientation, .63; independence, .58. Given the conditions under which the CBCL-2 was collected, the magnitude of these correlations is striking. They indicate a general consensus on the ratings among a considerable number of first and second grade teachers.

But the objection might be raised that these first and second grade teachers agreed so much because they had discussed the children beforehand and that the correlations represent the stability of stereotypes rather than the stability of behavior. This hypothesis would receive sup-

---

[21]With only a few exceptions, there was only one CD Project child in each of these elementary classrooms.

port if there were low correlations between ratings by preschool teachers and ratings by elementary school teachers, since the two groups of teachers had no opportunities to discuss the children with each other. To test this possibility, CBCL-2 factor ratings were regressed against POCL and CBCL-2 factor ratings of the same name. The multiple correlations obtained between ratings at preschool and grade 1 and between ratings at preschool and grade 2 appear in table 21. These correlations are similar in magnitude to those found between first and second grade ratings. They tend to discount the explanation of stereotype stability. Thus it appears that children's sociability, cooperation, and academic orientation as perceived by teachers were relatively stable from preschool through second grade.

Preschool program comparisons were also investigated for the CBCL-2 factor ratings. Analyses of variance comparing programs were carried out for CBCL-2 factor ratings at grades 1 and 2. The results of these comparisons appear in table 22. There were no significant differences across programs at grade 1, although there was a tendency for children from the Cognitive Program to be rated as more cooperative than children from the Language Program. At grade 2, the independence of children was rated as significantly different across programs. A post-hoc analysis with Scheffe confidence intervals ($p < .05$) showed that children from the Language Program were judged less independent than children from the other two programs. Dependency could have been fostered by the Language Program's teacher-centered approach; however, the existence of a tendency in the other direction at grade 1 makes the finding suspect.

# RELATIONSHIP BETWEEN TEACHER RATINGS AND NONPROGRAM CHILD VARIABLES

Teachers' ratings are important, not only for the information they provide on the children's classroom behavior, but also because of their potential ability to predict other child outcomes such as test scores. In addition, the presence of such predictable relationships between classroom behavior

**Table 21**

*Multiple Correlations Between Factor Ratings by Teachers at End of Preschool, Grade 1, and Grade 2*

| Predictors | Criterion | |
|---|---|---|
| POCL and CBCL-1 at Preschool | CBCL-2 at Grade 1 (n = 29) | CBCL-2 at Grade 2 (n = 28) |
| Sociability | .43 | .23 |
| Cooperation | .44 | .58** |
| Academic Orientation | .60** | .63** |

**p<.01.

**Table 22**

*Analyses of CBCL-2 Factor Ratings by Preschool Program*

| FACTOR | Grade | Program Means | | | F ratio |
|---|---|---|---|---|---|
| | | Cognitive | Language | Unit-Based | |
| Sociability | 1 | 4.33 | 3.52 | 3.94 | <1 |
| | 2 | 4.58 | 4.22 | 3.96 | <1 |
| Cooperation | 1 | 5.00 | 3.27 | 4.27 | 2.23 |
| | 2 | 4.25 | 3.89 | 4.25 | <1 |
| Academic | 1 | 3.46 | 3.20 | 3.05 | <1 |
| Orientation | 2 | 3.75 | 2.92 | 3.69 | <1 |
| Independence | 1 | 3.29 | 4.36 | 4.32 | <1 |
| | 2 | 4.44 | 2.92 | 4.88 | 4.64* |

NOTE: Sample size was as follows:

| | Cognitive | Language | Unit-Based | Total |
|---|---|---|---|---|
| Preschool | 11 | 15 | 15 | 41 |
| Grade 1 | 7 | 11 | 11 | 29 |
| Grade 2 | 8 | 12 | 8 | 28 |

*$p < .05$, $df = 2, 26$.

and test performance helps to establish the validity of the ratings themselves.

Before examining these relationships, it is important to determine whether ratings are biased by the sex or social class of the child. Although the three preschool curricula were balanced for sex and SES so that any biases would appear equally in the programs, the presence of any relationships between demographic and classroom behavior variables should be considered when examining relationships between test and behavior variables for the sample as a whole.

It was hoped that teacher ratings would not be greatly influenced by the child characteristics of sex and SES. The obtained product-moment correlations between these variables are presented in table 23. The only significant correlations are between sex and cooperation at preschool and again at grade 2. A multivariate analysis of variance, comparing ratings of boys and girls at all three time points, yielded a significant difference for cooperation, $F(4,13) = 4.02$, $p < .05$. Girls were rated as more cooperative than boys, a finding which appears often in the developmental literature (Maccoby & Jacklin, 1974). Apart from this relationship, however, teacher ratings of children appeared to be independent of children's demographic characteristics.

In order to examine the predictive and concurrent validity of teachers' ratings, achievement tests were chosen as a commonly accepted indicator of school success in the current educational system. One would expect that of the four factors rated, academic orientation would correlate most strongly with achievement scores. To the extent that cooperation with classroom procedures might also reflect a child's ability to learn what is taught in school, one could expect a moderate relationship between cooperation and achievement. No obvious predictions could be made, however, for correlations between independence or sociability and test scores.

The correlations presented in table 23 conform to these expectations. In fact, the magnitude of the correlations between academic orientation and achievement is striking. These correlations may be interpreted in a number of ways. Teachers' perceptions of children's classroom behavior may be influenced by their knowledge of children's performance on tests in general. Students who perform well on tests probably do show academically oriented behavior in the classroom (e.g., sustained attention) and teachers accurately perceive these characteristics. Further, children who exhibit such an orientation to learning may be favored by teachers and hence receive the individual attention which eventually results in higher test scores. Thus, these correlations probably reflect multidirectional in-

**Table 23**

*Correlations Between Classroom Ratings and Selected Nonprogram Variables*

| | Sex[1] | SES | California Achievement Test S1G | California Achievement Test S2G | Metropolitan Achievement Test[2] S4G |
|---|---|---|---|---|---|
| POCL and CBCL-1[3]: S2Y | | | | | |
| Sociability | .16 | .23 | .30 | .43* | .13 |
| Cooperation | .41* | .10 | .36 | .47* | .27 |
| Academic Orientation | .31 | .26 | .54** | .68** | .45* |
| CBCL-2: S1G | | | | | |
| Sociability | −.01 | −.13 | −.03 | .03 | .00 |
| Cooperation | .28 | .04 | .25 | .46* | .36 |
| Academic Orientation | .06 | −.12 | .44* | .58** | .58** |
| Independence | −.17 | −.12 | .29 | .18 | .35 |
| CBCL-2: S2G | | | | | |
| Sociability | .00 | −.03 | .22 | .33 | .08 |
| Cooperation | .40* | .02 | .35 | .41* | .34 |
| Academic Orientation | .20 | .05 | .52** | .52** | .48* |
| Independence | −.14 | −.11 | .33 | .07 | .14 |

NOTE:  S2Y = Spring, Second Year of Preschool
S1G = Spring, First Grade
S2G = Spring, Second Grade
S4G = Spring, Fourth Grade

[1] 1 = male; 2 = female

[2] Sum of 4 MAT subtests.

[3] Multiple correlations using POCL and CBCL-1 as predictors in a multiple regression formula. While multiple correlations are unsigned, both predictors were positive in each case.

*p<.05.

**p<.01 N = 37 to 41 at preschool, 26 to 29 thereafter.

fluences, rather than unidirectional causality. Nevertheless, they suggest that a relationship does exist between teachers' perceptions of children's classroom behavior and children's actual performance, supporting the concurrent and predictive validity of these ratings.

# RATINGS BY PARENTS

Parents of children in the CD Project were interviewed at length in the spring of their children's fourth-grade year. The Parent Interview focused on topics of potential relevance to the parent-child relationship, and how early educational intervention might have an impact on this relationship. It should be emphasized that this interview was constructed in conjunction with other longitudinal research at the High/Scope Foundation and that items were therefore not specifically designed to address curriculum-related outcomes.

Interviews were administered primarily to mothers and they responded to questions about themselves, fathers or male guardians, and their children. Questions combined structured, semi-structured and open-ended items, and covered the following four areas: demographic data, parents' interests and activities, parents' attitudes toward education, and parents' assessments of and relationships with their children. After all the interviews had been administered, response categories were created for the open-ended items, and interviews were then coded.

The interview questions of interest to the evaluation issues addressed in this study are parents' attitudes towards education and parents' relationships with their children. It is in these two realms that one might look for differential program impacts stemming from the child's involvement in preschool and from the involvement of both the parent (mother) and child in the home visits.

One-way analyses of variance comparing programs were performed on each of the interview items of interest. Of 146 variables analyzed, only two were significant at $p < .05$; it is possible that this number may have occurred by chance.

Parent Interview data, then, yielded few significant findings relative to the number of questions examined. It should therefore be concluded that the three preschool programs had no differential impact upon parents' subsequent attitudes about education or their relationships with their children. The possibility should be mentioned, however, that interview items designed to address potential curriculum-specific outcomes might have produced more significant findings.

# SUMMARY OF RATINGS BY TEACHERS AND PARENTS

Children's classroom behavior was rated by their teachers at the end of preschool and in the spring of first and second grade. Factor ratings were obtained at all three timepoints for children's academic orientation, coop-eration, and sociability. In addition, factor ratings on independence were derived in grades 1 and 2.

Because preschool teachers' ratings were based on comparisons of children within the same program, no meaningful comparisons across programs were possible. Primary grade teachers, however, were unaware of the particular curriculum treatment of the child(ren) they rated and were using broader standards of comparison; hence the three curricula could be compared on these later ratings. Finally, both the predictive validity of the preschool teachers' ratings and the concurrent validity of the primary teachers' ratings could be determined by examining their relationships with a measure of school success, i.e., achievement test scores.

Analyses showed no consistent program differences in children's rated classroom behavior in elementary school. Teachers' ratings were relatively independent of children's sex and socio-economic status. Ex-amining the relationship between preschool and elementary teachers' rat-ings and school success, predictably significant correlations were found between the factor of academic orientation and achievement test scores, supporting the concurrent and predictive validity of teacher ratings.

Parents of project children were interviewed when their children were in fourth grade. Responses dealing with parental attitudes towards education and parent-child relationships were analyzed for program dif-ferences. Few significant findings emerged.

In sum, there was little evidence that the three preschool programs produced differential effects on parental attitudes toward education or on how children were subsequently perceived by their teachers and parents during elementary school. Two explanations can be offered for these results. First, the characteristics assessed (e.g., academic orientation, par-ental attitudes towards the child and school) may indeed have been equally influenced by the three curricula. While differential methods were employed by the programs to enhance specific child skills or make parents more aware of various educational objectives, the outcomes for the children, their families, and their teachers may have been the same. Second, it is possible that the rating techniques used may not have been sensitive enough to pick up differences on these dimensions. Ideally, other measures (e.g., direct observation of interactions in elementary school classrooms or of parent-child relationships in the home) would have revealed differences between programs on these and other relevant variables. Since, however, such alternative assessment procedures were not feasible in this longitudinal evaluation, it is safest to conclude that the perceived classroom behaviors of children as well as the expressed educational attitudes of parents were not differentially affected by the three preschool programs.

In order to discover whether there were differential program impacts upon children's academic potential, standardized measures were ad-ministered to CD Project children both during and after preschool. Chap-ter V presents the results of this assessment.

# V Academic measures of children during and after preschool

Standardized aptitude and achievement test scores have often been misused in educational evaluation. None of the instruments employed in this study is presumed to measure a child's "general intelligence" or "innate ability." On the contrary, they are presumed to measure performance in tasks that are often developmentally and culturally inappropriate for poor and minority group children. The rationale for using these tests in the CD Project is two-fold. First, a standardized aptitude test is a good indicator of a program's impact per se on children's growth, i.e., it indicates whether a program is an effective one. Second, these tests are generally good predictors of performance in traditional academic settings, as they were designed to be. In fact, achievement test scores have become a major criterion of educational success in many school systems. Although the Cognitive and Unit-Based programs, in particular, sought to provide children with more than the ability to succeed in traditional academic settings, this evaluation focuses upon the relative effectiveness of each program in preparing children to succeed in the public schools. Consequently, test scores will be used to compare children in the sample with each other or with themselves over time, as well as to compare the three programs. Where data are available, comparisons will also be made with similar groups of disadvantaged children. Finally, in order to supplement the standardized instruments, children will be examined on a measure of "actual school success," i.e., their placement "on grade" in regular elementary programs as opposed to being retained in grade or referred for special education programs after they enter elementary school.

The results of testing on various cognitive and linguistic measures are presented in two parts in this chapter. First, findings on tests administered during the course of the three preschool programs are discussed. Second, longitudinal information on academic potential gathered during kindergarten, first, second, and fourth grade is presented. Table 24 summarizes the cognitive-linguistic data gathered at each of the testpoints before (FEY), during (SEY, S2Y), and after (SKG, S1G, S2G, S4G) preschool.

# ACADEMIC MEASURES DURING PRESCHOOL

Four instruments were administered to the children during the two years of the preschool program. Three of these instruments measured general aptitude or aspects of cognitive development: the Binet, PPVT, and Leiter. The fourth instrument, the ITPA, measured linguistic development. The Binet was the only test administered to all the children before they enrolled in preschool. As discussed in chapter II, these pretreatment Binet scores were used as one criterion in sample selection. All four instruments were administered to each child during the spring of the first and second year of preschool. The tests were administered individually by trained testers, and the same tester administered all four instruments to each child.

The Binet, PPVT, Leiter, and ITPA are each described below. This discussion is followed by a statement of the research questions addressed with these measures during preschool and the results obtained.

**Table 24**

*Cognitive-Linguistic Data*
*(collected at each testpoint before, during, and after preschool)*

| Before Preschool | During Preschool | | After Preschool | | | |
|---|---|---|---|---|---|---|
| FEY | SEY | S2Y | SKG | S1G | S2G | S4G |
| Binet | Binet | Binet | Binet | Binet | Binet | |
| | | | | | | WISC |
| | PPVT | PPVT | | | | |
| | Leiter | Leiter | | | | |
| | ITPA | ITPA | ITPA | ITPA | | |
| | | | | CAT | CAT | |
| | | | | | | MAT |
| | | | | Grade Placement | Grade Placement | Grade Placement |

## The Stanford-Binet Intelligence Scale, Form L-M, 1960 Edition (Binet)

**Description.**   The Binet is the oldest and most widely used test of general intelligence or aptitude. It is described fully in the examiner's manual by Terman and Merrill (1960). According to Sattler (1974), the Binet is preferable to the Wechsler Intelligence Scale for Children (WISC) because it provides better coverage at the lower age levels and provides a more reliable assessment at the extreme ranges.

**Reliability and validity.**   The test-retest reliability for the Stanford-Binet (1937 version) is .91, which establishes the Binet as one of the most reliable of all tests (Cronbach, 1960). In general, the Binet tends to be more reliable at higher ages and lower IQs (Anastasi, 1968).

Data on the criterion-related validity of the Stanford-Binet, both concurrent and predictive, have been obtained chiefly in terms of academic achievement. Earlier versions of the Binet have been correlated with school grades, teachers' ratings, and achievement test scores; most of these correlations fall between .40 and .75 (Anastasi, 1968). Few validation studies have been done with the 1960 Form L-M. Kennedy, Van de Reit, and White (1963) report a correlation of .69 with total score on the California Achievement Test in a large sample of Black elementary-school children. Follow-up data on children from the Perry Preschool Project (Weikart, Bond, and McNeil, 1978) indicate correlations of .44 to .63 between the Binet and the CAT in grades 1 to 4.

## The Peabody Picture Vocabulary Test (PPVT)

**Description.**   The PPVT was developed by Dunn to provide an estimate of a child's "verbal intelligence" through measurement of the child's receptive knowledge (hearing recognition) of vocabulary. A complete description of the PPVT is presented in Dunn (1965).

The PPVT scores presented in this report are ratio IQs (i.e., the ratio of mental age to chronological age), rather than deviation IQs based on the standard score norms in the examiner's manual (Dunn, 1965). The ratio IQ is used here because it can better differentiate IQ changes in one-month intervals over the nine-month school year. The PPVT deviation IQs are only given by six-month intervals and are thus not as sensitive to changes during short time periods.

**Reliability and validity.**    As reported in the test manual, reliability coefficients based on alternate forms ranged from .67 to .84. Reliability for the preschool ages covered in this report ranged from .72 to .82.

Validity was originally established in terms of age differentiation. Since its publication, the test has been employed in a number of studies with normal, mentally retarded, emotionally disturbed, and physically handicapped subjects. These studies have yielded validity coefficients in the .60s with individual and group aptitude scales within relatively homogeneous age groups. As expected, these correlations were higher with verbal than with performance tests. There is also some evidence of moderate concurrent and predictive validity in correlations with academic achievement tests (Anastasi, 1968; Weikart, Bond, and McNeil, 1978).

## Arthur Adaptation of the Leiter International Performance Scale (Leiter)

**Description.**    A general description of the Leiter is included in the examiner's manual (Arthur, 1952; Leiter, 1959). The test was designed as a nonverbal Binet scale for children between three and eight years old, although the similarity of items is not always obvious. The Leiter consists of 40 items covering 10 age levels from 2 years to just over 12 years. Many of the items are perceptual in nature, requiring the child to match identical colors, designs, or pictures. As the items progress in difficulty, they call for such operations as design completion, number matching, matching by genus, matching by use, progressive series sequencing, quantity estimation, and matching people by age. The test is administered by pantomime in order to be completely unbiased by the child's language ability.

**Reliability and validity.**    The reliability of the Leiter for different age levels is not presented in the test manuals. Sharp (1958), using a six-month test-retest procedure with 48 retarded children, obtained a reliability coefficient of .91. Spellacy and Black (1972) report a 25-week test-retest reliability coefficient of .86 for a group of language-impaired children.

The validity of the Leiter is generally assessed by its correlation with the Binet. Orgel and Dreger (1955) reported correlations of .67 to .75 for different samples from a standard population. Weikart, Deloria, Lawser, and Wiegerink (1970) administered the Leiter and the Binet to a sample of lower SES Black children. They found the correlations between the two tests to increase from .25 at three years old to .55 at eight years old. None of the correlations were high enough to demonstrate equivalence between the two tests. The correlation between the Leiter and the Binet for all the children in the CD Project was .55 in the spring of the first year of preschool and .32 in the spring of the second year. Thus, the Leiter is not redundant with the Binet as a test of general aptitude, particularly with economically disadvantaged populations.

## Illinois Test of Psycholinguistic Abilities, Revised Edition, 1968 (ITPA)

**Description.**    A general description of the revised edition of the ITPA is contained in the examiner's manual (Kirk, McCarthy, and Kirk, 1968). The ITPA has been used to delineate areas of difficulty in communication, to diagnose specific cognitive disabilities, and to test general aptitude.

In this study, four of the twelve ITPA subtests were selected as specific measures of language performance. These four subtests were selected for two reasons: (1) in the Perry Preschool Project (Weikart et al., 1970) they were found to measure a practical range of language behaviors, i.e., children were able to attain a basal age; and (2) they measured performance at the representational level. The four subtests are as follows:

*Grammatic Closure*—This required the child to present the correct grammatic completion of an incomplete phrase, e.g., "Here's a dog; here are two _____."

*Auditory Association*—This is a verbal analogies test, e.g., "I cut with a saw; I pound with a _____."

*Verbal Expression*—This measures the child's capacity to verbally describe several familiar objects; e.g., the child is given a ball and asked to "tell me all you know about this." Responses are scored for the number of concepts expressed, such as the object's name, shape, usage, size, and other classifying properties, and their relevancy to the stimuli.

*Auditory Reception*—This measures the child's ability to comprehend verbally presented material, e.g., "Do dials yawn?" Responses may be a simple yes or no, or even a nod of the head.

In addition to scores on the four individual ITPA subtests, an "ITPA Subset Score" has been computed by averaging the four ITPA scaled scores for each child. This subset score is used to determine the child's overall ability to use standard or "mainstream" language. It is important that this subset score not be confused with the ITPA Composite Score or Mean Scaled Score, which are summary scores of the 10 main subtests or the 12 total ITPA subtests.

All of the ITPA analyses in this study used scaled scores rather than language-age scores. The scaled scores are standardized within age levels with a mean of 36 and a standard deviation of 6. This standardization permits comparisons of subtests with each other, and comparison of subtest scores with themselves over time (Paraskevopoulos and Kirk, 1969).

**Reliability and validity.** According to Carroll (1972), the technical characteristics of the ITPA appear highly satisfactory. However, Paraskevapoulos and Kirk (1969) report the following test-retest reliabilities for the four subtests used in this study:

| | Restricted Range Stability Coefficient[22] | Full Range Estimates[23] |
|---|---|---|
| Grammatic Closure | .56 | .72 |
| Auditory Association | .71 | .90 |
| Verbal Expression | .45 | .74 |
| Auditory Reception | .56 | .79 |

The validity of the ITPA when used with minority or lower SES populations has been questioned by many authors (Waddell and Cahoon, 1970; Severson and Guest, 1970; Howard, Hoops and McKinnon, 1970). The implications of the doubtful validity of the ITPA are summarized by Carroll (1972), who states that "the use of the ITPA in evaluating the effects of language programs for the disadvantaged is highly questionable, unless one views the purpose of such testing as that of finding out how much these programs advance the child toward certain middle-class language norms." (p. 823) Although the ITPA cannot be considered a valid measure of functional language ability for the minority group and lower SES children in this study, it does provide a measure of children's ability to use standard language as required in the formal school setting.

# Concurrent research questions & results

The three questions addressed with the measures of cognitive-linguistic development collected during the preschool period are as follows:

- What was the extent of improvement over all groups combined in measured cognitive development during preschool?
- Did the three programs have differential impact on the extent to which children improved in measured cognitive and linguistic development during preschool?
- Which children benefited most from each of the three programs during preschool?

## Overall gains in cognitive development during preschool

Overall gains in cognitive development during preschool were assessed with the Binet since this was the only measure on which pretreatment

---

[22]One entire age range of 71 children who were four years old.

[23]Full-range estimate of reliability based on the 71 four-year-olds tested for the restricted stability coefficient, after correction for restricted intelligence.

scores were available. Table 25 presents the results of a repeated measures analysis of variance of Binet scores comparing programs from the fall to the spring of entering year (FEY to SEY). Table 26 presents repeated measures analysis of variance results from the fall of the entering year to the spring of the second year of preschool (FEY to S2Y).

The highly significant trials main effect in both tables indicates that one of the important results of the CD Project was the large overall gain in cognitive development during preschool as measured by the Binet. At the end of one year of preschool, the three groups combined gained an average of 23.5 points in Binet IQ. By the end of the second year this gain had decreased somewhat, but was still an average 16.8 points for the children as a whole. A control group of children from the Perry Preschool Project, selected on the same criteria as the CD Project children but receiving no preschool treatment, gained 4.8 and 0.2 Binet points, respectively, during the equivalent one- and two-year periods (Weikart et al., 1978). Using these Perry control group gains as an indication of change due to regression toward the mean, the Binet gains made by the CD children in the three programs combined represent educationally, as well as statistically, significant cognitive growth.

## Group comparisons of cognitive-linguistic development during preschool

At the end of the first year of preschool, children in the three programs were quite similar in their scores on cognitive and linguistic measures. As table 26 indicates, Binet scores during SEY and changes in Binet scores from FEY to SEY were not significantly different for the three curricula. Table 27 presents results of one-way analyses of variance comparing groups, for the PPVT, Leiter, and ITPA subtests at SEY. Again, no significant group differences emerged for six out of the seven measures of cognitive-linguistic development. Scheffe post-hoc comparisons on the one significant difference indicated that Unit-Based children scored significantly lower on the ITPA Auditory Reception Subtest than children in the other two programs. With this one exception then, children in the three curricula were quite similar in cognitive-linguistic development at the end of the first year of preschool.

By the end of the second year of preschool, significant program differences emerged on one linguistic and two cognitive measures. Post-hoc comparisons on the significant group and interaction effects presented in table 27 indicated that Binet scores in the Language Program were significantly higher than those in the other two programs by the end of the second preschool year. Pretreatment (FEY) Binet scores were quite similar for the three groups, so that higher scores for the Language group represent greater increases in Binet performance. Further, as can be seen from looking at the SEY and S2Y testings, Binet scores in all three curricula dropped from spring of the first year to spring of the second year. The Language group, however, did not decrease as much as the Cognitive and Unit-Based groups, accounting for the greater net gains among Language Program children. The relative increases and decreases

**Table 25**

*Group by Trials Analysis of Variance of Stanford-Binet Scores: FEY to SEY*

| GROUP | FEY Mean | FEY S.D. | FEY N | SEY Mean | SEY S.D. | Mean Difference FEY to SEY | Group Main Effect F Ratio | Trials Main Effect F Ratio | Group by Trials Interaction F Ratio |
|---|---|---|---|---|---|---|---|---|---|
| Cognitive[1] | 80.1 | 6.97 | 10 | 103.5 | 13.87 | +23.4 | | | |
| Language | 81.9 | 5.82 | 15 | 106.9 | 13.17 | +25.0 | | | |
| Unit-Based | 79.7 | 7.49 | 15 | 102.1 | 7.39 | +22.4 | <1 | 201.5** | <1 |
| Three Groups Combined | 80.7 | 6.67 | 40 | 104.2 | 11.44 | +23.5 | | | |

[1]One child in the Cognitive group was not tested at SEY. Since only children having both tests are presented here, see table 27 for complete FEY data.

**p<.01.

**Table 26**

*Group by Trials Analysis of Variance of Stanford-Binet Scores: FEY to S2Y*

| GROUP | FEY Mean | FEY S.D. | FEY N | S2Y Mean | S2Y S.D. | Mean Difference FEY to S2Y | Group Main Effect F Ratio | Trials Main Effect F Ratio | Group by Trials Interaction F Ratio |
|---|---|---|---|---|---|---|---|---|---|
| Cognitive | 80.5 | 6.77 | 11 | 94.5 | 12.07 | +14.0 | | | |
| Language | 81.9 | 5.82 | 15 | 105.5 | 12.11 | +23.6 | | | |
| Unit-Based | 79.7 | 7.49 | 15 | 92.0 | 8.51 | +12.3 | 4.70* | 101.08** | 4.70* |
| Three Groups Combined | 80.8 | 6.62 | 41 | 97.6 | 12.28 | +16.8 | | | |

*p<.05.
**p<.01.

in group means on the Binet at these three testpoints (FEY, SEY, and S2Y) are illustrated in figure 13.

Table 28 presents results of one-way analyses of variance comparing groups for the other cognitive and linguistic measures administered at the end of the second year of preschool. Two of the seven analyses showed a significant group effect. Post-hoc comparisons indicated that PPVT scores in the Language Program were significantly higher than those in the

**Figure 13**

*Group Means on Binet Scores Before and During Preschool*

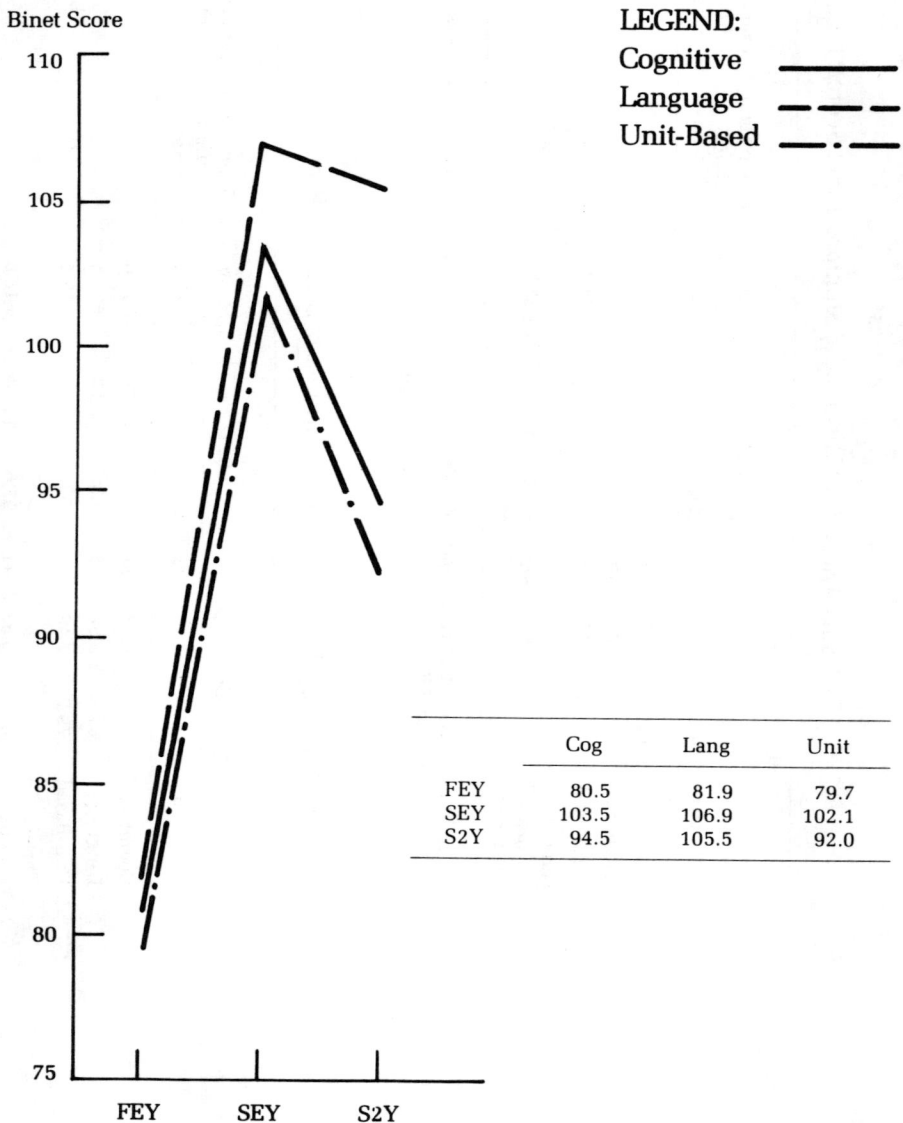

|  | Cog | Lang | Unit |
|---|---|---|---|
| FEY | 80.5 | 81.9 | 79.7 |
| SEY | 103.5 | 106.9 | 102.1 |
| S2Y | 94.5 | 105.5 | 92.0 |

**Table 27**

One-Way Analyses of Variance of PPVT, Leiter, and ITPA Subtests at SEY

| Test | Cognitive | | | Language | | | Unit-Based | | | F Ratio |
|---|---|---|---|---|---|---|---|---|---|---|
| | N | Mean | S.D. | N | Mean | S.D. | N | Mean | S.D. | |
| PPVT | 10 | 75.9 | 14.46 | 14 | 83.3 | 12.33 | 15 | 80.3 | 12.81 | < 1 |
| Leiter | 10 | 102.6 | 25.11 | 15 | 115.7 | 16.71 | 15 | 105.9 | 19.59 | 1.52 |
| ITPA—Grammatic Closure Subtest | 10 | 33.7 | 6.38 | 14 | 31.5 | 5.80 | 14 | 29.0 | 4.40 | 2.18 |
| ITPA—Auditory Association Subtest | 10 | 34.1 | 5.34 | 14 | 34.7 | 5.68 | 14 | 31.9 | 5.55 | 1.01 |
| ITPA—Verbal Expression Subtest | 10 | 31.2 | 5.77 | 14 | 35.1 | 6.52 | 14 | 31.0 | 4.06 | 2.31 |
| ITPA—Auditory Reception Subtest | 10 | 36.6 | 4.16 | 14 | 35.9 | 4.01 | 14 | 32.5 | 3.72 | 3.67* |
| ITPA—Subset Score | 10 | 33.8 | 3.94 | 14 | 34.3 | 4.24 | 14 | 31.1 | 3.55 | 2.66 |

**Table 28**

One-Way Analyses of Variance of PPVT, Leiter, and ITPA Subtests at S2Y

| Test | Cognitive | | | Language | | | Unit-Based | | | F Ratio |
|---|---|---|---|---|---|---|---|---|---|---|
| | N | Mean | S.D. | N | Mean | S.D. | N | Mean | S.D. | |
| PPVT | 11 | 86.2 | 19.76 | 15 | 99.5 | 21.30 | 15 | 78.5 | 13.08 | 5.07* |
| Leiter | 11 | 95.9 | 12.46 | 15 | 101.5 | 11.96 | 15 | 97.8 | 16.85 | < 1 |
| ITPA—Grammatic Closure Subtest | 11 | 34.0 | 5.55 | 15 | 33.9 | 7.57 | 14 | 29.4 | 8.30 | 1.78 |
| ITPA—Auditory Association Subtest | 11 | 32.5 | 6.15 | 15 | 33.6 | 6.38 | 15 | 27.7 | 6.31 | 3.70* |
| ITPA—Verbal Expression Subtest | 11 | 33.5 | 6.88 | 15 | 33.5 | 5.67 | 15 | 31.4 | 6.14 | < 1 |
| ITPA—Auditory Reception Subtest | 11 | 33.2 | 3.12 | 15 | 33.3 | 3.09 | 15 | 33.3 | 4.53 | < 1 |
| ITPA—Subset Score | 11 | 33.3 | 4.18 | 15 | 33.6 | 4.32 | 15 | 30.5 | 5.19 | 2.02 |

*p < .05.

Unit-Based Program. PPVT scores for the Cognitive Program fell in between the Language and Unit-Based programs and were not significantly different from either. On linguistic measures, the lower performance of Unit-Based children on the ITPA Auditory Reception Subtest at the end of the first year had disappeared by the end of the second year. However, Unit-Based children did score significantly lower than Language children on the ITPA Auditory Association Subtest. As with the PPVT, scores of Cognitive children were intermediate and not significantly different from the other two programs, although they were closer to the higher scores of the Language group.

Although all three programs were similar at the end of the first preschool year, at the end of the two years of preschool children in the Language Program had higher scores on two measures of cognitive-linguistic development. Scores of children in the Language Program did not drop as much during the second year as those of Cognitive and Unit-Based children. This may be attributable to the programmed style of the Language Curriculum, where children are required to respond in "correct," predetermined ways to fast-paced demands from the teachers. This response style is also appropriate to the testing situation. Language Program children might have been expected to score relatively higher than children from the other two programs on the ITPA subtests, especially the Grammatic Closure and the Auditory Association subtests, which focus on language usage. The emphasis of the Cognitive Program on relational language, however, could also account for the similar scores of these two groups on the Auditory Association Subtest. Even though the Language and Cognitive groups tended to score slightly higher than the Unit-Based Program on the ITPA subtests, the three groups were generally quite similar. The fact that only a few significant differences did emerge on these linguistic measures probably reflects the fact that language development was stressed to a large extent in all three curricula.

## Children who benefited most from each of the three programs during preschool

An important concern of educators and educational policy-makers is whether various types of preschool programs are differentially effective for different children. Although the CD Project can provide no definitive answer to this question, some consideration of the issue in light of the available data seems worthwhile. Restating the question in terms of this study:

> Were the three programs differentially effective for children who entered at different ability levels or who were from families of different socio-economic status?

The research question was addressed by interacting entering characteristics and treatment group membership in multiple linear regressions to predict cognitive and linguistic scores in the spring of the first and second year of preschool. Entering ability was measured by Stanford-Binet performance prior to enrollment (FEY); entering socio-economic status was assessed with the SES index described in the beginning of chapter II. The dependent measures in these interaction analyses were the Binet, PPVT, Leiter, and ITPA scores obtained during preschool.

Of the 32 regression analyses performed, only one was significant at $p < .05$ (program interacted with FEY Binet scores to affect SEY Binet scores), and this finding may have occurred by chance. In general, the absence of any other significant interactions suggests that the three programs were equally effective in developing children's cognitive-linguistic abilities (over the rather narrow range of aptitude and socio-economic status represented in the CD sample).

## Summary of findings on academic measures obtained during preschool

- There was a large overall gain in cognitive development, as measured by Binet scores, during the first year of preschool. Although these gains decreased somewhat by the end of the second preschool year, they still represented a large and significant improvement over pre-treatment scores for all groups combined.

- The three groups were quite similar to each other on most cognitive-linguistic measures, particularly at the end of the first preschool year. By spring of the second year, children in the Language Program scored significantly higher than those in the other two programs on the Binet, and significantly higher than Unit-Based children on the PPVT. Despite a tendency for Unit-Based children to score lower than the other groups on some ITPA subtests, few significant group differences emerged in linguistic development during preschool.

- The three programs were equally effective for children who entered at different ability levels or who came from families of different socio-economic status.

# ACADEMIC MEASURES AFTER PRESCHOOL

Following preschool, no treatment intervention occurred for either the children or their mothers other than the few hours needed each spring to complete tests, ratings, or interviews. Academic measures were administered to the children at four testpoints: in the spring of kindergarten, first, second, and fourth grades (SKG, S1G, S2G, and S4G). The Stanford-Binet was administered through S2G; the WISC was administered at S4G. The decision to use the WISC at grade 4 rather than continue to use the Binet was based on the fact that data analyses through grade 2 had revealed no program differences in children's IQ scores. It was hoped that the WISC, which provides subscores on a number of cognitive-linguistic tests, would be more sensitive to educational treatment effects than the single, more global IQ score obtained with the Binet.

In addition to the Binet or WISC, the following instruments were used at each of the four testpoints: SKG—ITPA; S1G—ITPA and CAT;

S2G—CAT; and S4G—MAT. The decision to use the MAT for the fourth-grade testing rather than continue to use the CAT was based primarily on expediency and a desire to cooperate with the schools. The Ypsilanti Public Schools, which most children from the CD Project were still attending, administered the MAT to all fourth graders in their classrooms. In order to avoid giving the sample children a second achievement test and to spare teachers and children the disruption of an additional testing session, MAT scores were obtained from school records.

All the cognitive-linguistic measures were collected from the children in the schools in which they were currently enrolled. The Binet, WISC, and ITPA were administered individually by trained testers; the CAT was given by a High/Scope Foundation staff member to small groups of children; the MAT was administered by teachers in the classroom for most children and by a staff member to small groups of children who were attending school in nearby school districts. The CAT and the MAT were each administered in two 90-minute sessions in order to avoid tiring the children.

Instruments used to collect longitudinal data on children's cognitive, linguistic, and achievement skills are described below. This is followed by a statement of the research questions addressed with these measures after preschool and the results obtained. A final section examines the impact of preschool as a whole, and each of the three programs separately, on the actual school success (i.e., regular grade and program placement versus retention or special education) of the children.

The Stanford-Binet and the ITPA are described in the preceding section. The WISC and the two achievement tests, the CAT and the MAT, are described here.

## The Wechsler Intelligence Scale for Children, 1949 (WISC)

**Description.** The WISC is a downward extension of the Wechsler-Bellevue Intelligence Scale used with adolescents and adults. It is described fully in the examiner's manual by Wechsler (1949). The WISC differs from the Binet in two fundamental ways. First, the WISC abandons the concept of "mental age." Instead, a deviation IQ is computed by comparing each subject's test performance, not with a composite age group, but exclusively with the scores earned by individuals in the subject's own age group. The IQ of 100 on the WISC is thus set equal to the mean total score for each age. Second, the WISC is based on the belief that general intelligence is not a unitary trait or ability. For this reason, the WISC is made up of 10 tests, all equally weighted. Five of these tests constitute the Verbal Scale; five constitute the Performance Scale. The Verbal and Performance scores together make up the Full Scale Score. Correlations in the .80s have been found between Full Scale IQs and Verbal and Performance IQs.

Raw scores are converted to scale scores on the WISC so that they are standardized and can be treated arithmetically (i.e., added). The scaled scores were standardized with a mean of 10 and a standard deviation of 3 at each age for each of the separate tests. IQs, also derived separately for each age, have a mean of 100 and a standard deviation of 15 for the standardization sample. This mean and standard deviation was predetermined for the Verbal IQ and the Performance IQ as well as the Full Scale IQ.

**Reliability and validity.** The reliability coefficients of the individual tests and of the Verbal, Performance, and Full Scale Scores are presented below for ages 7½ and 10½. Reliabilities were computed as follows: for coding, alternate forms of the test were given to 7½-year-olds only; for composite scores (Verbal, Performance, and Full Scale Scores), sums of odd and even items were correlated; for all other test scores, the Spearman-Brown split-half technique was used.

| | Reliability Coefficients | |
| --- | --- | --- |
| | Age 7½ | Age 10½ |
| Information | .66 | .80 |
| Comprehension | .59 | .73 |
| Arithmetic | .63 | .84 |
| Similarities | .66 | .81 |
| Vocabulary | .77 | .91 |
| Verbal Score | .88 | .96 |
| Picture Completion | .59 | .66 |
| Picture Arrangement | .72 | .71 |
| Block Design | .84 | .87 |
| Object Assembly | .63 | .63 |
| Coding | .60 | — |
| Performance Score | .86 | .89 |
| Full Scale Score | .92 | .95 |

Although subtest reliabilities ideally might be higher, reliabilities for the Full Scale, Verbal, and Performance IQs appear to be sufficiently reliable for most testing purposes. Longitudinal data indicate that WISC IQs are about as stable as Stanford-Binet's over a four-year interval (Gehman and Matyas, 1956). When 60 fifth-grade pupils were retested in the ninth grade, their Stanford-Binet IQs correlated .78. On the WISC, the Full Scale, Verbal, and Performance IQs correlated .77, .77, and .74, respectively.

Correlations between the WISC and the Binet vary widely with the age, aptitude level, and heterogeneity of the samples, but the majority are in the .80s. The Verbal Scale correlates more highly with the Binet than does the Performance Scale. Normal and superior children tend to score lower on the WISC than on the Stanford-Binet (Littell, 1960). The discrepancy in favor of the Binet is greater for higher scoring and for younger subjects. For the mentally retarded, the WISC yields a significantly higher mean IQ than the Binet. Since all previous elementary-grade testings with the Curriculum Demonstration sample show them to be within the normal range (i.e., Binet means in the middle to high 90s), and since the WISC is being used with nine-year-olds in this study rather than with very young children, WISC IQs should be closely related to Binet IQs.

### The California Achievement Tests, 1957 Edition, 1963 Norms, Lower Primary, Form W (CAT)

**Description.** A complete description of the CAT is provided in the examiner's manual (Tiegs & Clark, 1963). The CAT is used to measure each child's academic skills. It is composed of three subtests covering the areas of reading, arithmetic, and language. Each of these three subtests is divided into two parts, as follows:

*Reading Subtest:* reading vocabulary and reading comprehension

*Arithmetic Subtest:* arithmetic reasoning and arithmetic fundamentals

*Language Subtest:* mechanics of English and spelling

Raw scores for each CAT subtest were computed by adding raw scores from the two parts. The CAT total raw score was obtained by summing all three subtest raw scores. Only raw scores are used in the analyses in this study.

**Reliability and validity.** As reported in the examiner's manual, test-retest reliability coefficients for Reading, Arithmetic, Language, and Total Score are .88, .90, .86, and .95, respectively. North (1965) reports reliabilities for the subtest and total scores to range from .86 to .96. He does caution, however, that reliabilities for some of the individual parts that make up the subtests fell below .80 on the Lower Primary level. None of the part scores are analyzed individually in this report.

Information provided by Tiegs and Clark (1963) also suggests that the CAT has adequate content and construct validity as assessed by the correlation of CAT subtest scores with children's performance on other achievement tests.

### The Metropolitan Achievement Tests, Elementary, Form F, 1970 (MAT)

**Description.** A complete description of the MAT is provided in the teacher's handbook (Durost, Bixler, Wrightstone, Prescott, and Balow, 1971). The MAT consists of seven tests—two which can be combined into a Total Reading score; Language; Spelling; and three which can be combined into a Total Mathematics score:

*Total Reading:* word knowledge and reading comprehension

*Language:* syntax, punctuation, and capitalization

*Spelling:* writing words spoken by examiner

*Total Mathematics:* computation, concepts, and problem-solving

Raw scores for each test are computed by adding the total number of correct answers. The four raw scores used in this study—Total Reading, Language, Spelling, and Total Mathematics—are computed by adding all the test scores that comprise each of these four areas. In addition, an MAT Total Score is computed by adding the raw scores on all the tests. As with the CAT, only raw scores are used in these analyses.

**Reliability and validity.**  The teacher's handbook reports the following split-half and test-retest reliability coefficients for each of the MAT tests administered in the fall of grade 4:

| Test | Split-Half | Test-Retest |
|------|------------|-------------|
| Word Knowledge | .94 | .95 |
| Reading | .92 | .93 |
| Total Reading | .96 | .97 |
| Language | .93 | .93 |
| Spelling | .96 | .97 |
| Mathematics Computation | .88 | .91 |
| Mathematics Concepts | .90 | .91 |
| Mathematics Problem-Solving | .91 | .93 |
| Total Mathematics | .96 | .97 |

Reliabilities for the test scores used in this study are quite high, ranging from .93 to .97. The test's authors do not claim that the MAT has universal content validity. They say rather that each school must determine the MAT's content validity in the light of its own curriculum.

**Suitability for disadvantaged children.**  As reported in the teacher's handbook, standardization samples were selected to represent the national population in terms of geographical region, size of city, socioeconomic status, and public versus nonpublic schools. The socioeconomic index was based on median family income and median years of schooling for adults in the community. Norms are based on the standardization sample as a whole and are not reported separately by region, SES, etc. As with the CAT, this national sample does not provide information specific to disadvantaged or minority populations. Therefore, raw scores rather than percentile ranks are used in this study, and analyses compare treatment groups with each other rather than with national samples.

# Longitudinal research questions & results

The three questions addressed with the longitudinal cognitive-linguistic measures collected after preschool parallel those asked during the preschool period:

- What was the extent of longitudinal impact over all groups combined in measured cognitive development?

- Did the three programs have differential longitudinal impact on children's measured cognitive and linguistic development during the five years after preschool?

- Which children benefited most from each of the three preschool programs after they entered the elementary grades?

## Overall gains in cognitive development after preschool

As table 29 indicates, there were no further gains in aptitude scores over and above the gains recorded at the end of preschool. However, the gains that were made during preschool were maintained during the first five years of elementary school. Even as late as fourth grade, WISC scores remain as high as earlier Binets. This is particularly impressive since children in the normal IQ range tend to score lower on the WISC than on the Binet (Littell, 1960). As shown in tables 30 through 33, the trials main effect from FEY (before preschool) to SKG, S1G, S2G, and S4G, respecitvely (after preschool) is highly significant each year. The gains over pretreatment IQ scores for all three groups combined were 14.9, 16.4, 13.1, and 14.7 for SKG, S1G, S2G, and S4G, respectively.

The longitudinal aptitude scores for the CD sample follow a pattern similar, but not identical, to the Binet scores of the Perry Preschool experimental group (Weikart, Bond, and McNeil, 1978). The mean Binet score for Perry experimental children was 94.7 at the end of preschool and had gradually dropped to 85.1 by the fourth grade. Experimental-group Binet means had ceased being significantly different from control-group means by spring of the second grade. The mean Binet score for children in the CD Project was 97.6 at the end of preschool and their mean WISC score was 95.7 in the spring of fourth grade. Thus, the CD Project children did not drop nearly as much in measured IQ during this period as the experimental children from the Perry Project. IQ scores of children in the CD Project compared to those of children in the Perry control group are significantly higher at each timepoint up to and including fourth grade.

The consistency of IQ scores in this study can be further addressed by correlating Binet scores during preschool, Binet scores during early elementary school, and WISC scores in the middle of elementary school. Table 34 presents these correlations. They show that Binet scores at preschool (FEY) are unrelated to subsequent IQ scores both during and after preschool attendance. It would seem that the impact of these preschool programs was not associated with entering ability, so that children with a wide range of initial abilities could potentially benefit from being involved in preschool. However, IQ scores at the end of the first year of preschool (SEY) are positively and consistently correlated with IQ scores at all subsequent testpoints through fourth grade. That is, once aptitude gains had been made during the entry year, these improvements dropped

**Table 29**

*IQ Scores at the End of Preschool and After Preschool
for All Groups Combined*

| Testpoint | Test | N | Mean IQ | S.D. |
|-----------|------|---|---------|------|
| S2Y | Binet | 41 | 97.6 | 12.28 |
| SKG | Binet | 35 | 95.5 | 14.25 |
| S1G | Binet | 41 | 97.2 | 13.03 |
| S2G | Binet | 40 | 94.1 | 13.65 |
| S4G | WISC | 36 | 95.7 | 14.14 |

**Table 30**

*Repeated Measures Analysis of Variance of Stanford-Binet Scores: FEY to SKG*

| GROUP | FEY Mean | FEY S.D. | N | SKG Mean | SKG S.D. | Mean Difference FEY to SKG | Group Main Effect F Ratio | Trials Main Effect F Ratio | Group by Trials Interaction F Ratio |
|---|---|---|---|---|---|---|---|---|---|
| Cognitive[1] | 80.4 | 6.71 | 9 | 95.9 | 17.39 | +15.5 | | | |
| Language[1] | 82.0 | 6.04 | 14 | 98.0 | 15.94 | +16.0 | < 1 | 38.44** | < 1 |
| Unit-Based[1] | 79.1 | 7.67 | 12 | 92.3 | 9.37 | +13.2 | | | |
| Three Groups Combined | 80.6 | 6.72 | 35 | 95.5 | 14.25 | +14.9 | | | |

[1]Some children from each group were not tested at SKG. Since only children having both tests are presented here, see table 26 for complete FEY data.

**p < .01.

**Table 31**

*Repeated Measures Analysis of Variance of Stanford-Binet Scores: FEY to S1G*

| GROUP | FEY Mean | FEY S.D. | N | S1G Mean | S1G S.D. | Mean Difference FEY to S1G | Group Main Effect F Ratio | Trials Main Effect F Ratio | Group by Trials Interaction F Ratio |
|---|---|---|---|---|---|---|---|---|---|
| Cognitive | 80.5 | 6.77 | 11 | 94.9 | 16.36 | +14.4 | | | |
| Language | 81.9 | 5.82 | 15 | 99.3 | 13.38 | +17.4 | < 1 | 64.31** | < 1 |
| Unit-Based | 79.7 | 7.49 | 15 | 96.7 | 10.27 | +17.0 | | | |
| Three Groups Combined | 80.8 | 6.62 | 41 | 97.2 | 13.03 | +16.4 | | | |

**p < .01.

**Table 32**

*Repeated Measures Analysis of Variance of Stanford-Binet Scores: FEY to S2G*

| GROUP | FEY Mean | S.D. | N | S2G Mean | S.D. | Mean Difference FEY to S2G | Group Main Effect F Ratio | Trials Main Effect F Ratio | Group by Trials Interaction F Ratio |
|---|---|---|---|---|---|---|---|---|---|
| Cognitive | 80.5 | 6.77 | 11 | 94.6 | 16.36 | +14.1 | | | |
| Language | 81.9 | 5.82 | 15 | 96.0 | 13.38 | +14.1 | | | |
| Unit-Based[1] | 80.4 | 7.35 | 14 | 91.6 | 11.97 | +11.2 | < 1 | 31.71** | < 1 |
| Three Groups Combined | 81.0 | 6.52 | 40 | 94.1 | 13.65 | +13.1 | | | |

[1]One child in the Unit-Based group was not tested at S2G. Since only children having both tests are presented here, see table 26 for complete FEY data.

**p < .01.

**Table 33**

*Repeated Measures Analysis of Variance of Stanford-Binet Scores: FEY to S4G*

| GROUP | FEY Mean | S.D. | N | S4G Mean | S.D. | Mean Difference FEY to S4G | Group Main Effect F Ratio | Trials Main Effect F Ratio | Group by Trials Interaction F Ratio |
|---|---|---|---|---|---|---|---|---|---|
| Cognitive[1] | 81.4 | 6.48 | 10 | 96.2 | 16.02 | +14.8 | | | |
| Language | 81.9 | 5.82 | 15 | 98.3 | 13.80 | +16.4 | | | |
| Unit-Based[1] | 79.4 | 8.08 | 11 | 91.5 | 13.13 | +12.1 | < 1 | 13.33** | < 1 |
| Three Groups Combined | 81.0 | 6.65 | 36 | 95.7 | 14.14 | +14.7 | | | |

[1]Some children from the Cognitive and Unit-Based groups were not tested at S4G. Since only children having both tests are presented here, see table 26 for complete FEY data.

**p < .01.

**Table 34**

## IQ Correlations across All Testpoints

|      | FEY    | SEY    | S2Y    | SKG    | S1G    | S2G    |
|------|--------|--------|--------|--------|--------|--------|
| SEY  | .42**  |        |        |        |        |        |
| S2Y  | .36*   | .77**  |        |        |        |        |
| SKG  | .24    | .78**  | .65**  |        |        |        |
| S1G  | .24    | .70**  | .64**  | .77**  |        |        |
| S2G  | .18    | .59**  | .70**  | .71**  | .76**  |        |
| S4G  | .29    | .76**  | .74**  | .75**  | .73**  | .72**  |

*p < .05.
**p < .01.

some but then remained relatively stable until the end of preschool and into grades K, 1, 2, and 4.

It can thus be concluded that an important result of the CD Project was the large increase in Binet scores during preschool and the consistent maintenance of these higher IQ scores during the first five years of elementary school for all three treatment groups combined.

## Group comparisons of cognitive-linguistic development after preschool

A major result which recurs in all of the group comparisons during the first five years of elementary school is that there were almost no significant differences between the three treatment groups.

Longitudinal differences in cognitive development were best assessed in this study using aptitude (Binet and WISC) scores because a pretreatment measure was available, as well as subsequent testings. Four repeated measures analyses of variance comparing the three programs were performed on IQ scores at FEY to SKG, FEY to S1G, FEY to S2G, and FEY to S4G. Tables 30 through 33 present these results. No group main effect and no group by trials interaction was found in any of the analyses. The only significant finding was the trials main effect discussed in the previous section for all groups combined. Figure 14 presents the mean IQ scores for each group at all testpoints, i.e., before, during, and after preschool. This figure emphasizes the finding that although the Language group scored significantly higher than the other two groups at the end of preschool, these differences on the Binet disappeared by kindergarten and did not reappear on either the Binet or the WISC during this follow-up study. If gain scores from FEY are examined in tables 30 through 33, the differences between the programs are even smaller. It should be noted, however, that the Language group's aptitude scores were the highest (though nonsignificantly) at all testpoints, and with the exception of first grade, the Unit-Based scores were the lowest. The reasons for this consistent pattern are not apparent. It is possible that one group has a slight advantage or disadvantage relative to the other groups on certain components (e.g., verbal skills) common to all the IQ tests, which is in turn manifested in this trend of differential group performances in overall aptitude scores. The following examination of the WISC and its component tests addresses this explanation.

As stated earlier, the WISC was administered in fourth grade with the expectation that scores on the various WISC tests might reveal program differences which the unitary Binet scores and the Full Scale WISC IQ masked. One-way analyses of variance, by group, were therefore performed on the WISC Verbal IQ, Performance IQ, and the 10 separate tests which comprise the WISC IQ scores. Table 35 presents these results.

**Figure 14**

*Group Means on IQ Scores Before, During, and After Preschool*

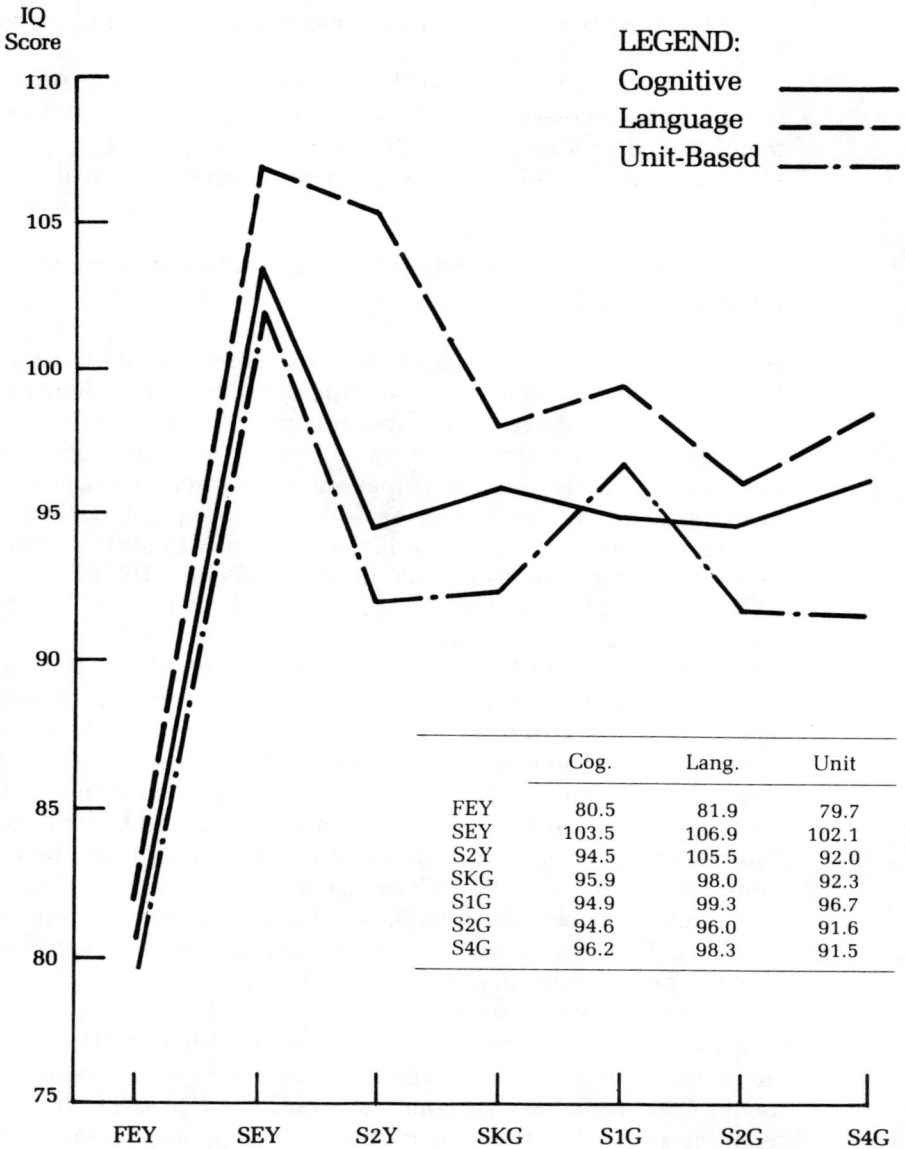

LEGEND:
Cognitive ——————
Language — — — —
Unit-Based —— · ——

|  | Cog. | Lang. | Unit |
|------|------|-------|------|
| FEY | 80.5 | 81.9 | 79.7 |
| SEY | 103.5 | 106.9 | 102.1 |
| S2Y | 94.5 | 105.5 | 92.0 |
| SKG | 95.9 | 98.0 | 92.3 |
| S1G | 94.9 | 99.3 | 96.7 |
| S2G | 94.6 | 96.0 | 91.6 |
| S4G | 96.2 | 98.3 | 91.5 |

Only one test, Comprehension, showed a significant group effect. Post-hoc comparisons indicated that children in the Cognitive Program scored significantly higher (p<.05) than those in the Unit-Based Program. Language group scores were intermediate and not significantly different from the other two groups. This result is consistent with the goals of the Cognitive Curriculum; that program's emphasis on reasoning out the "what" and "why" of phenomena could account for the subsequent higher performance on this test of comprehension. If this finding does reflect program impact, it is striking that this effect would still show up five years after preschool terminated. Unfortunately, we have no longitudinal data on comprehension which traces relative reasoning ability in the three curriculum groups at each year subsequent to preschool intervention.

None of the other IQ or scaled test scores showed a significant treatment effect. Further, no consistent rank ordering of the three programs emerged across the 10 WISC tests. However, for the five tests which comprise the Verbal Scale, the Unit-Based always scored below the Cognitive and Language programs. This may reflect a more systematic, if not a greater, emphasis on verbal skills (including arithmetic) in the Language and Cognitive programs. In addition, the (nonsignificantly) lower verbal scores of the Unit-Based children relative to the other two groups may account for their (nonsignificantly) lower total aptitude scores at almost all testpoints.

Linguistic development was assessed in kindergarten and first grade with the ITPA. Table 36 presents one-way analyses of variance for the four ITPA subtests and the subset score at SKG and at S1G. No significant group differences were found on any of the ITPA measures. Thus, the few significant differences which showed the Unit-Based group to be behind the other groups in linguistic development during preschool had disappeared by the time the children were in kindergarten and first grade. Again, the absence of group differences on linguistic measures is best explained by the emphasis placed on language development in all three curricula. Even though the nature and consistency of this emphasis was different in the three programs, its effectiveness in helping children use standard language appears to have been equal.

Academic achievement was assessed by the CAT in first and second grade. Table 37 presents the one-way analyses of variance by group for raw scores on the CAT subtests and the CAT total score at S1G and S2G. Academic achievement was measured with the MAT in fourth grade. Table 38 presents the one-way analyses of variance by group for raw scores on the four MAT tests and the MAT total score. No significant group differences were found on any of the achievement subtests or total scores at any of the three testpoints.

Table 39 presents the rank orderings of the three groups on achievement test reading, mathematics, language, and total scores in the spring of first, second, and fourth grades. No consistent rank ordering emerges for reading, mathematics, or total scores across the three testpoints. Total scores, however, do show the same rank ordering at the two later testpoints, i.e., Cognitive>Language>Unit-Based at S2G and S4G, and this may indicate a stabilization of overall achievement patterns as children get older. Continued testing at subsequent grades would be needed

**Table 35**

One-Way Analyses of Variance of WISC Verbal IQ, Performance IQ, and Scaled Test Scores

| WISC Variable | Cognitive (N=10) | | Language (N=15) | | Unit-Based (N=11) | | F Ratio |
|---|---|---|---|---|---|---|---|
| | Mean | S.D. | Mean | S.D. | Mean | S.D. | |
| Verbal IQ: | 96.9 | 15.01 | 94.7 | 14.24 | 86.7 | 12.44 | 1.61 |
| Information | 8.8 | 2.49 | 7.7 | 2.41 | 7.6 | 2.66 | < 1 |
| Comprehension | 9.8 | 2.49 | 8.2 | 2.65 | 6.7 | 2.24 | 4.00* |
| Arithmetic | 9.2 | 3.43 | 8.3 | 2.50 | 7.7 | 2.72 | < 1 |
| Similarities | 10.8 | 2.82 | 11.9 | 3.50 | 9.4 | 2.69 | 2.08 |
| Vocabulary | 8.9 | 3.25 | 9.7 | 2.29 | 8.0 | 3.29 | 1.05 |
| Performance IQ: | 96.2 | 15.56 | 102.8 | 13.58 | 98.7 | 15.37 | < 1 |
| Picture Completion | 8.8 | 2.25 | 9.1 | 2.58 | 8.9 | 2.12 | < 1 |
| Picture Arrangement | 10.7 | 3.59 | 11.1 | 3.74 | 8.4 | 2.58 | 2.29 |
| Block Design | 8.8 | 2.25 | 9.5 | 2.29 | 9.5 | 4.55 | < 1 |
| Object Assembly | 8.7 | 2.98 | 11.7 | 3.06 | 10.5 | 5.09 | 1.94 |
| Coding | 10.3 | 3.65 | 10.5 | 2.47 | 11.8 | 3.46 | < 1 |

*p < .05.

**Table 36**

One-Way Analyses of Variance of ITPA Subtests at SKG and S1G

| Test | Test-point | Cognitive | | | Language | | | Unit-Based | | | F Ratio |
|---|---|---|---|---|---|---|---|---|---|---|---|
| | | N | Mean | S.D. | N | Mean | S.D. | N | Mean | S.D. | |
| ITPA—Grammatic Closure Subtest | SKG | 9 | 30.4 | 8.81 | 13 | 30.5 | 7.76 | 12 | 26.2 | 4.61 | 1.43 |
| | S1G | 11 | 30.1 | 5.20 | 15 | 30.9 | 7.20 | 13 | 27.5 | 6.46 | 1.07 |
| ITPA—Auditory Association Subtest | SKG | 9 | 28.8 | 6.44 | 13 | 28.9 | 7.47 | 12 | 26.0 | 4.77 | < 1 |
| | S1G | 11 | 30.1 | 5.05 | 15 | 30.3 | 7.09 | 13 | 29.8 | 5.06 | < 1 |
| ITPA—Verbal Expression Subtest | SKG | 9 | 33.9 | 1.76 | 13 | 36.5 | 7.49 | 12 | 30.6 | 6.45 | 2.90 |
| | S1G | 11 | 34.9 | 4.21 | 15 | 35.7 | 5.42 | 13 | 33.8 | 5.64 | < 1 |
| ITPA—Auditory Reception Subtest | SKG | 9 | 30.8 | 6.82 | 13 | 34.5 | 6.12 | 12 | 31.9 | 5.66 | 1.11 |
| | S1G | 11 | 32.4 | 6.34 | 15 | 33.9 | 5.78 | 13 | 29.3 | 4.68 | 2.35 |
| ITPA—SUBSET SCORE | SKG | 9 | 31.0 | 4.87 | 13 | 32.6 | 4.73 | 12 | 28.7 | 3.15 | 2.67 |
| | S1G | 11 | 31.9 | 3.22 | 15 | 32.7 | 4.39 | 13 | 30.1 | 4.18 | 1.51 |

**Table 37**

*One-Way Analyses of Variance of CAT at S1G and S2G*

| Test | Test-point | Cognitive | | | Language | | | Unit-Based | | | F Ratio |
|---|---|---|---|---|---|---|---|---|---|---|---|
| | | N | Mean | S.D. | N | Mean | S.D. | N | Mean | S.D. | |
| CAT—Reading Subtest | S1G | 11 | 47.2 | 16.09 | 15 | 41.6 | 17.40 | 14 | 48.4 | 12.13 | < 1 |
| | S2G | 11 | 66.3 | 17.11 | 15 | 60.1 | 19.60 | 12 | 60.2 | 13.42 | < 1 |
| CAT—Arithmetic Subtest | S1G | 11 | 46.6 | 20.18 | 15 | 44.3 | 20.83 | 14 | 54.9 | 13.47 | 1.29 |
| | S2G | 11 | 69.4 | 17.31 | 15 | 64.1 | 18.90 | 12 | 57.3 | 22.86 | 1.07 |
| CAT—Language Subtest | S1G | 11 | 28.4 | 14.22 | 15 | 22.5 | 10.06 | 14 | 25.9 | 10.93 | < 1 |
| | S2G | 11 | 47.5 | 18.41 | 15 | 37.1 | 17.70 | 12 | 39.0 | 15.52 | 1.22 |
| CAT—TOTAL RAW SCORE | S1G | 11 | 121.4 | 49.27 | 15 | 107.3 | 42.44 | 14 | 129.2 | 29.97 | 1.04 |
| | S2G | 11 | 183.1 | 48.88 | 15 | 160.5 | 49.93 | 12 | 156.7 | 45.83 | 1.01 |

**Table 38**

*One-Way Analyses of Variance of MAT at S4G*

| Test | Cognitive (N=10) | | Language (N=15) | | Unit-Based (N=13) | | F Ratio |
|---|---|---|---|---|---|---|---|
| | Mean | S.D. | Mean | S.D. | Mean | S.D. | |
| MAT Total Reading | 50.40 | 19.32 | 52.33 | 16.52 | 39.89 | 16.34 | 2.17 |
| MAT Spelling | 22.20 | 9.33 | 20.73 | 9.39 | 21.23 | 9.26 | < 1 |
| MAT Language | 18.70 | 11.79 | 13.80 | 9.84 | 16.54 | 13.16 | < 1 |
| MAT Total Mathematics | 55.20 | 24.18 | 57.73 | 18.10 | 53.84 | 23.46 | < 1 |
| MAT TOTAL RAW SCORE | 146.50 | 60.42 | 144.60 | 42.55 | 130.54 | 54.78 | < 1 |

to see if this pattern is in fact stable.

The only consistent rank ordering across all testpoints was on language scores, i.e., Cognitive>Unit-Based>Language. This finding is certainly surprising. One would not predict from curricular models that Language Program children would score below those in the other two groups on measures of language achievement which stress mechanics of English (sentence formation, punctuation) and spelling. Possibly the Language Program children became used to the systematized drill during preschool and could not adapt to their elementary school teachers' methods of language instruction, or possibly they were "turned off" by the constant drill during preschool and hence "tuned out" during subsequent language teaching in elementary school. As with total achievement scores, however, additional testing would be needed to substantiate any language achievement patterns across the three programs. Further, it should be stressed again that none of the group differences in any of the achievement subtests or total scores were significant at any of the three testpoints during elementary school.

In summary, children from the three programs were significantly different from each other on only one (the WISC Comprehension) of the 28 cognitive-linguistic measures analyzed after preschool. If we set alpha at .05, we should recognize that this difference may have occurred by chance.

## Children who benefited most from each of the three programs after preschool

The same question addressed above for the preschool period is addressed here using outcome measures obtained after preschool:

> Were the three programs differentially effective for children who entered at different ability levels (FEY Binet) or who were from families of different socio-economic status?

The research question was addressed with the same multiple linear regression design used to assess differential program effectiveness during preschool. Treatment group membership was interacted with pretreatment Binet scores and with entering SES to predict post-treatment (kindergarten, first, second, and fourth grade) Binet, WISC, ITPA, CAT, and MAT scores.

Of the 98 regression analyses performed, only four were significant at $p<.05$: program interacted with FEY Binet scores to affect ITPA Auditory Association and CAT Arithmetic; program interacted with entering SES to affect WISC Arithmetic and WISC Object Assembly scores. Post-hoc comparisons yielded no consistent patterns upon which to base a conclusion that one program was more beneficial for a given type of child than the other programs. Given the overwhelming number of nonsignificant interactions, these analyses suggest that the three preschool curricula were equally effective for children who entered at different ability levels or came from families of different socio-economic status, at least over the range of ability and SES represented in the CD sample.

## Actual school success

In addition to standard aptitude and achievement tests, another, more concrete, measure of school success was used to evaluate the overall effectiveness of the three preschool programs as well as the relative impact of each. Data were obtained at each spring testing in elementary school (grades 1, 2, and 4) on every child's grade and program placement, i.e., "on grade" versus "retained" versus "placed in special education." Table 40 presents the cumulative number of children in each program, and in all three programs combined, who were retained in grade or placed in special education at each of these grades.

To assess the effectiveness of preschool attendance *per se* on the actual school success of the children, the results must be examined relative to a comparable control group that did not attend any preschool. As discussed earlier in regard to IQ gains for the three CD groups combined, the experimental and control groups in the Ypsilanti Perry Preschool Project were similar to the CD sample in entering characteristics (Binet and socio-economic status). Following are the percentages of children either retained in grade or placed in special education as of grade 4 for the CD sample as a whole, and for the Perry experimental and control groups (Weikart, Bond, and McNeil, 1978):

| | |
|---|---|
| CD—all groups combined (N=41) | 19.5% |
| Perry experimental group (N=58) | 17.0% |
| Perry control group (N=65) | 38.0% |

As these percentages indicate, approximately half as many children who attended one of the three CD preschools or the Perry Preschool were retained in grade or placed in special education by fourth grade as control group children.

To examine the relative school success of children who had attended the three preschool programs, a one-way analysis of variance by group was performed[24] on the number of children either retained or placed in special education through fourth grade. No significant group effect was found ($F(2,38)=0.01$, $p<.99$); this result parallels the findings on aptitude and achievement measures.

# Summary of findings on academic measures obtained after preschool

- There were no further gains in aptitude scores, as measured by the Binet and the WISC, over and above those gains recorded at the end of preschool. The gains that were made during preschool, however, continued to be maintained through the fourth grade. The sample as a whole showed an average gain of 15 points in aptitude scores from pretreatment to fourth grade testing.

---

[24]Children placed "on grade" were assigned scores of 0; children retained in grade or placed in special education were assigned scores of 1.

**Table 39**

*Rank Orderings of Groups on Achievement Scores at S1G, S2G, and S4G*

| Achievement Variable | Testpoint | | |
|---|---|---|---|
| | S1G | S2G | S4G |
| Reading | Unit > Cog > Lang | Cog > Unit > Lang | Lang > Cog > Unit |
| Mathematics | Unit > Cog > Lang | Cog > Lang > Unit | Lang > Cog > Unit |
| Language (including Spelling) | Cog > Unit > Lang | Cog > Unit > Lang | Cog > Unit > Lang |
| TOTAL SCORE | Unit > Cog > Lang | Cog > Lang > Unit | Cog > Lang > Unit |

**Table 40**

*Cumulative Number of Children Retained in Grade or Placed in Special Education*

| Group | N | Grade 1 | | Grade 2 | | Grade 4 | | TOTAL |
|---|---|---|---|---|---|---|---|---|
| | | Retained | Spec. Ed. | Retained | Spec. Ed. | Retained | Spec. Ed. | Retained or Spec. Ed. |
| Cognitive | 11 | 0 | 0 | 1 | 0 | 2 | 0 | 2 |
| Language | 15 | 1 | 0 | 2 | 0 | 2 | 1 | 3 |
| Unit-Based | 15 | 1 | 0 | 1 | 0 | 3 | 0 | 3 |
| Three Groups Combined | 41 | 2 | 0 | 4 | 0 | 7 | 1 | 8 |

■ There were almost no significant differences between the three treatment groups on cognitive-linguistic measures administered during the first five years of elementary school. In aptitude measures, no program differences emerged on total Binet or WISC scores, although the Language group tended to score higher than the other two. The only significant difference, which may have occurred by chance, was in WISC Comprehension at grade 4—scores of children who had been in the Cognitive Program were higher than those of children from the Unit-Based Program. On linguistic (ITPA) measures no significant differences were found. Further, on achievement (CAT and MAT) measures, no significant group differences were found, although the Cognitive group tended to score the highest and the Language group the lowest.

■ The three programs were equally effective for children who entered at different ability levels or who came from families of different socio-economic status.

■ Approximately one out of five children in the CD Project sample were either retained or placed in special education programs by the fourth grade. This number is close to the occurrence of retention or special education placement found for a comparable group of children who participated in the Ypsilanti Perry Preschool Project. Comparing both of these samples with the control group from the Perry Preschool study, it appears that children who attended a preschool program had twice as much "actual school success" (i.e., half as many retentions and special education referrals) as children who did not participate in a preschool program. No significant differences were found among the three CD programs in terms of the percentage of children who succeeded in school according to this measure.

# VI Summary, discussion & conclusions

# SUMMARY

The Curriculum Demonstration Project was designed to compare the effectiveness, under carefully controlled experimental conditions, of three theoretically distinct approaches to compensatory preschool education. This chapter reviews the outcomes and discusses the implications of the project.

## Design of the project

### Three preschool programs were compared: a cognitive program, a language program, and a unit-based or traditional program.

The three programs compared in this study represent the major approaches to early childhood education in operation during the late 1960s. The *Cognitively Oriented Curriculum* is an "open framework" approach developed by High/Scope staff in the Ypsilanti Perry Preschool Project (Weikart, 1967). Piaget's theory provided the foundation for this model, which is based on the assumption that mental growth occurs through children's active exploration and manipulation of their environment. The *Language Training Curriculum* is a "programmed" approach adapted from the work of Bereiter and Engelmann (1966). In this model, the academic problems of economically disadvantaged children are viewed as stemming from inadequate language development. Direct, programmed instruction is used to provide children with specific pre-academic skills in an atmosphere of "friendly competition" and positive reinforcement. The *Unit-Based Curriculum* is a "child centered" approach based on traditional nursery school programs. The focus is on the social and emotional growth of the child, and teachers are guided by their own intuition and general knowledge of child development in formulating the curriculum.

### Three- and four-year-old children, identified as economically disadvantaged and academically high-risk, attended preschool for two years.

The study involved 41 children, about equally divided among the three programs. The children were from families of low socio-economic status living in Ypsilanti, Michigan. Their Stanford-Binet scores prior to preschool were low, with a mean of 81 points. Children entered the project in two waves, one wave beginning in 1967 and the other in 1968. Each child entered preschool as a three-year-old and remained in the program for two years.

### Noncurriculum variables were carefully controlled so that outcomes could be attributed to program-related effects.

The basic administrative parameters of the three programs were essentially the same. All children attended half-day preschool sessions, five days a week, for two school years. A team of teachers, assisted by an adult aide and a student helper, was responsible for each classroom, and the staff/child ratio (excluding helpers) was maintained at 1 to 5. All three teaching teams were closely supervised and engaged in separate daily planning and evaluation sessions. In addition, teachers made home visits every two weeks, each visit lasting about 90 minutes, during which mothers were encouraged to help their children learn at home using methods consistent with their children's preschool program.

**The effectiveness of each of the three curricula was examined both concurrently during the two years of the preschool program and longitudinally by following up children through the fourth grade.**

Program impact was assessed with measures of cognitive and linguistic development, socio-emotional behavior, academic achievement, and grade placement. Cognitive ability was measured with the Binet before and during preschool, and through second grade. The Arthur Adaptation of the Leiter and the Peabody Picture Vocabulary Test (PPVT) were also administered during preschool, and the Wechsler Intelligence Scale for Children (WISC) was used at fourth grade. Linguistic development was assessed during preschool and kindergarten with subtests of the Illinois Test of Psycholinguistic Abilities (ITPA). Academic achievement was measured with the California Achievement Test (CAT) in grades 1 and 2 and the Metropolitan Achievement Test (MAT) at grade 4. Teachers completed behavior ratings of the children during preschool and in first and second grade. Parents were interviewed when children were in the fourth grade. Children's grade and special-education placement were determined at each data collection point during elementary school.

# Documentation of the programs

**Program processes were carefully documented to verify that the CD Project was, in fact, a curriculum comparison study.**

Three observational methods were used to verify the implementation of the three program models. First, classroom behavior was systematically observed using the Pupil Record of School Experience (PROSE) developed by Medley, Schluck, and Ames (1968b). Second, classrooms were observed by 12 consultants who were nationally recognized experts in child development and early childhood education. Third, teachers described the home setting and recorded their activities in their Home Visit Reports.

**Teachers represented programs rather than idiosyncratic teaching styles.**

Over the course of the project, anywhere from two to five teachers were responsible for implementing each curriculum model. Observational documentation of programs indicated that, in all cases, activities conducted by teachers within the same program were much more similar than those conducted by teachers from different programs. This finding supports the conclusion that the CD Project compared curricula rather than teachers.

**The three programs implemented three distinct curriculum models.**

In the Language Program, or programmed approach, adults verbally directed groups of children in academic tasks. There was little spontaneous social interaction among the children themselves. The Cognitive Program, or open framework approach, was characterized by teachers interacting with children, both individually and in small groups, to support learning at the child's own level of cognitive development. In the Unit-Based Program, or child-centered approach, the emphasis was on socio-emotional growth and self-expression. Children in this program engaged in fantasy play and divergent activities.

## Impact during preschool

**There was a large overall gain in cognitive development, as measured by the Binet, during preschool.**

At the end of the first year of the program, the three groups combined had an average Binet score of 104, a gain of 23 points over their entry level. By the end of the second year of preschool, the average gain had dropped to 17 points but was still statistically greater than combined aptitude scores before preschool.

**Children in all three programs were quite similar to each other on cognitive-linguistic measures at the end of the first year of preschool. At the end of the second year, children in the Language Program had significantly higher aptitude scores.**

The Binet scores of the Language Program children did not drop as much during the second year of preschool, resulting in higher scores relative to the other two programs. PPVT scores of Language children were also significantly greater than those of Unit-Based children at the end of the program. Despite a tendency for Unit-Based children to score lower than Cognitive and Language children on some ITPA subtests, few significant differences emerged in linguistic development during preschool.

**The three programs were equally effective during preschool for children with varying entry characteristics.**

Children who entered the project at different ability levels or who came from families of different socio-economic status benefited equally from the Language, Cognitive, and Unit-Based programs in measured cognitive growth.

## Impact after preschool

**The large cognitive gains evident for the group at the end of preschool were still being maintained five years after the children entered elementary school.**

Binet scores at the end of preschool averaged 98 points; WISC scores at the end of fourth grade averaged 96 points. The 15-point gain from pretreatment to fourth-grade testing is not only statistically significant but also represents a meaningful increase in children's academic potential.

**Children who participated in the CD Project were only half as likely to be retained in grade or placed in special education as a comparable group of children who had not attended preschool.**

Approximately one out of five children in the CD sample were not in their regular grade or class by the fourth grade. This number is close to the occurrence of retention or special-education placement of experimental-group children who participated in the Ypsilanti Perry Preschool Project. Comparing both of these samples with the Perry control group, it appears that the children who attended these preschool programs have had much greater "actual school success" (i.e., regular grade and class placement) than the children who did not attend a preschool program.

**Children who received home visits during their two years of preschool scored significantly higher on standardized achievement tests than children who attended preschool but did not have home visits.**

Achievement test scores of children who received home visits (i.e., Waves 6 and 7 analyzed in this report) were compared with those of children who did not receive home visits (i.e., Wave 8, which, as explained in chapter II, was not included in other analyses in this report). Results indicated that CD Project children who had home visits scored significantly higher on the first-grade CAT and fourth-grade MAT than those who did not have this home teaching component in their preschool program.

**There were almost no significant differences between children in the three programs on cognitive measures administered during the first five years of elementary school (K-4).**

One significant difference in aptitude scores did emerge, however: children in the Cognitive Program scored higher than those in the Unit-Based Program on WISC Comprehension at grade 4. Although no other aptitude measures showed significant group differences, Language Program children tended to score highest and Unit-Based children lowest on the Binet and WISC.

**Grade placement and linguistic and achievement measures administered after preschool also did not reveal any significant differences in program impact.**

Children in the three programs were not significantly different in rates of grade retention or special-education placement, nor in scores of linguistic development or academic achievement. There was a tendency, however, for Cognitive Program children to score the highest and Language Program children the lowest on the ITPA, CAT, and MAT.

**No consistent or meaningful program differences emerged in elementary school teachers' ratings of children's behavior or parents' responses to interview questions at fourth grade.**

Items composing the rating scales and interviews were not designed to assess potential curriculum-related differences. Actual differences may have emerged with more sensitive instruments.

**The three programs were equally effective through fourth grade for children with varying entry characteristics.**

Children who entered preschool at different ability levels or who came from families of different socio-economic status benefited equally from the Language, Cognitive, and Unit-Based programs in maintaining cognitive growth.

# DISCUSSION

## Review of other preschool curriculum comparison studies

The initial group of preschool studies beginning in the early 1960s addressed the question of the effect of preschool *versus* no preschool on the growth and development of young children. (See Beller, 1973, for a broad summary.) The Ypsilanti Perry Preschool Project has been examining that question. A second group of studies beginning about 1968 examined the effects of different preschool curricula on children. The Ypsilanti Preschool Curriculum Demonstration Project represents that type of study. In a sense, the second group of studies offers a competition between models based on different theories of child development and learning. This section will look at major studies in this second group, including Karnes (1973) study at the University of Illinios; Miller and Dyer's (1975) study of four preschool programs in a public-school setting in Louisville, Kentucky; and National Planned Variation Head Start, operated by the Office of Child Development, with eight model sponsors in a range of ethnic and geographic centers throughout the country. The major dimensions of these studies are diagrammed in figure 15. Several other studies, not reviewed here, have also been concerned with the differential effects of distinct curriculum models, among them Palmer (1976) and Smith and James (1975).

In the Karnes project, a sample of children from the Champaign-Urbana community was assigned to five classrooms the first year, and a second sample was assigned to three of these classrooms the second year. Each classroom represented a specific model program. The five models were as follows: 1) A traditional nursery program where the staff sought to promote personal, social, emotional, and general language development in the children; 2) a community-integrated program with a traditional nursery school experience, where the disadvantaged children were scattered to four middle-class neighborhood centers; 3) a Montessori program

**Figure 15**

## Dimensions of Curriculum Comparison Studies

| Domain | Dimensions | Curriculum Demonstration (1967-70) | Karnes (1965-67) | Miller and Dyer (1968-69) | PVHS (1969-72) |
|---|---|---|---|---|---|
| Project Characteristics | Scope of Project | Demonstration | Demonstration | City | National |
| | Curriculum Models: | | | | |
| | Programmed (Academic) | Language | Direct Verbal | Bereiter-Engelmann | Kansas, Oregon and Pittsburgh |
| | Open Framework | Cognitive | Ameliorative | Darcee | High/Scope, NYU[a] and Far West Lab |
| | Child-Centered | Unit-Based | Community-Integrated Montessori | Traditional Montessori | Bank Street, Tucson REC[a], EDC[a], Florida Enabler |
| | Total Number of Models | 3 | 5 | 4 | 12 |
| | Control Group | — | — | X | X |
| | Number of Years of Preschool | 2 | 1 | 1 | 1 |
| | Programs with Regular Home Visits | all | none | some | some |
| Sample Characteristics | Total Experimental Sample Size (N) | 41 | 123 | 214 | 6000 |
| | Homogeneous (disadvantaged/high risk only) | X | — | X | — |
| | Heterogeneous (including non-disadvantaged and/or non-high risk) | — | X | — | X |
| Longitudinal Follow-up | Public school: | | | | |
| | Regular classes | X | X | X | X |
| | Intervention classes (grade K and/or Follow Through) | — | X | X | X |
| | Grade at last reported follow-up | G4 | G3[b] | G2 | no data |

| | | 81 | 95 | 92 | 91[c] |
|---|---|---|---|---|---|
| **Aptitude Findings** | Mean entry score for sample | | | | |
| | Net IQ gain at end of preschool: | | | | |
| | Programmed | 24 | 13 | 5 | 2 to 8[c] |
| | Open Framework | 14 | 14 | 0 | 3 to 24[c] |
| | Child-Centered | 12 | 8.5,6 | 6.5 | -2 to 8[c] |
| | Control | — | — | 2 | -1 to 7[c] |
| | Net IQ gain at last reported follow-up: | | | | |
| | Programmed | 16 | 8 | -6 | no data |
| | Open Framework | 15 | 7 | -5 | no data |
| | Child-Centered | 12 | 6[b] | 0.1 | no data |
| | Control Group | — | — | 4 | no data |
| **Achievement Findings** | Group(s) significantly higher at end of preschool: | | | | |
| | Reading | no data | no differences | Open Framework Child-Centered (Montessori only) | Programmed[c] |
| | Mathematics | no data | Programmed Open Framework | Open Framework Child-Centered (Montessori only) | Programmed[c] |
| | Group(s) significantly higher at last reported follow-up: | | | | |
| | Reading | no differences | Open Framework[b] | Child-Centered (Montessori only) Programmed | no data |
| | Mathematics | no differences | no differences[b] | Control Child-Centered | no data |

[a]NYU = New York University
REC = Responsive Environments Corporation
EDC = Educational Development Corporation

[b]Data are not yet available for two child-centered programs (Community-Integrated and Montessori) in the Karnes study.

[c]PVHS data reported in this table refer to the second year (1970-71) only. Aptitude data do not include one Open Framework (NYU) and one Child-Centered (Enabler) model. Achievement data do not include one Open Framework (NYU) model.

staffed by teachers who met the local Montessori society's standards; 4) Karnes' Structured Cognitive program, a psycholinguistic model, built from the Illinois Test of Psycholinguistic Abilities, that provided opportunities for verbalization in conjunction with manipulation of materials in small groups; and 5) the Bereiter-Engelmann program, where the staff provided intensive oral drill in verbal and logical patterns to small groups. Karnes directed the Traditional and Structured Cognitive programs. The others were operated by their own staffs independent of Karnes.

This project was similar to the CD Project in several ways. Like the CD Project it included a traditional program and the Bereiter-Engelmann program. (There was no exact parallel to the Cognitive Program of the CD Project.) Both projects also included children described as "high risk disadvantaged," although Karnes' group of children was more heterogeneous, including children who were disadvantaged but not at risk. In both projects, the researcher responsible for the overall evaluation ran at least part of the project. Geographically, there is much similarity between the Urbana-Champaign area and the Ann Arbor-Ypsilanti area in terms of industry, education, and general population characteristics.

The Karnes study offers one of the few examples of curriculum comparison where there were some indications of both initial impact and positive long-term outcomes. The Bereiter-Engelmann and Structured Cognitive programs had, respectively, 13- and 14-point Binet gains at the end of preschool. Of the initial five models, only three were followed up into the third grade. Karnes (1973) reports that the Structured Cognitive program, the Traditional program, and the Bereiter-Engelmann program were not significantly different in measured Stanford-Binet aptitude scores, with all three approximately six points above entry scores. This score is about the same as the gain for the control group in the Ypsilanti Perry Preschool Project, which started with much lower entry levels, and about two points higher than the Miller and Dyer control-group gain (see below). It most likely represents the impact of both a program effect and some "school effect." (Bloom, 1964, p. 196, uses the term "freshman effect.") On reading achievement, Karnes' data indicate that the Karnes Structured Cognitive program was slightly but significantly higher than the Bereiter-Engelmann program and the Traditional program, both of which had above average scores.

On nonstandard measures, Karnes reports higher levels of motivation among children in the Structured Cognitive and Bereiter-Engelmann programs; she suggests that the emphasis on positive reinforcement in these programs was beneficial to the children's development of positive attitudes toward school. However, longitudinal investigation indicated that these initial differences were not maintained. Other findings on nonstandardized measures were that inventiveness was consistently low in children from the Bereiter-Engelmann program, and the curiosity of those who attended the Traditional program was consistently low into the early elementary grades. In regard to socio-emotional development, Karnes concludes that her Structured Cognitive program resulted in social gains that were equal to or greater than those made by children in the Traditional program. This was true despite the fact that the latter (like the Unit-Based in the CD Project) expressly viewed the acquisition of social skills as one of its primary goals.

The Miller and Dyer (1975) study focused on prekindergarten children in Louisville, Kentucky. The study sample was drawn from entering Head Start children and then "randomly distributed into experimental or non-experimental classes." (p. 14) The programs selected for the study were 1) the Bereiter-Engelmann program as used in both the Karnes study and the CD Project; 2) the Darcee (Demonstration and Research Center for Early Education) program developed by Susan Gray and co-workers at Peabody College, a model with no direct parallel in either the Karnes or the CD Project; 3) a Montessori program, again a parallel with Karnes but not with the CD Project; and 4) traditional programs reflecting the official Head Start position on preschool education and paralleling, to a great extent, the Karnes Traditional and Community-Integrated programs and the Unit-Based program in the CD Project. All curricula in the preschool year were under the general supervision of the project's research staff, a partial parallel with the CD Project. Unlike the Karnes study, in which some groups continued special intervention programs into kindergarten, the Miller and Dyer groups attended regular kindergarten classes (as did the CD groups).

The Miller and Dyer study reflects a problem that is common to other preschool education studies: program effects are not strong enough to be statistically significant. For example, the control group was the only group to show an increased aptitude score (of almost four points) from prekindergarten fall testing to the end of grade 2, the last available testpoint on the Stanford-Binet. This outcome is in part a typical "school effect" and is anticipated as part of attendance in a stimulating program. The treatment groups varied from "no gain-no loss" for the Traditional and Montessori programs to a five-point loss for Darcee and a six-point loss for children in the Bereiter-Engelmann program. While the study has a diminishing sample cell size and provides little information on the differential impacts of the various models, it does offer a wide range of ideas for hypothesis generation (e.g., program differences in "divergent thinking").

The largest nationwide study to date comparing various curriculum models was Planned Variation Head Start (PVHS) (Datta, 1976; Bissell, 1973; Smith, 1973; Weisberg, 1973), which was instituted in 1969 with eight model sponsors and 16 sites. The next year the number of sites was expanded to 37, and three new model sponsors were added. Some of the sites implemented their own models without any outside sponsorship. In spite of its problems as a research study (e.g., Rivlen and Timpane, 1975), PVHS represents a serious national effort to answer important questions regarding curriculum outcomes. The purpose of the project was to demonstrate the relative effectiveness of various curriculum models in diverse settings throughout the country. The models employed included the Engelmann-Becker program (evolved from the original Bereiter-Engelmann program), which was represented in the Miller and Dyer, Karnes, and CD projects; programs of the Educational Development Corporation, Bank Street College, and Enabler (the last providing support for local projects by trained early childhood education specialists committed to the goals of traditional preschool education), which parallel the Unit-Based Curriculum in the CD Project and the traditional programs in both the Miller and Dyer and Karnes projects; and the High/Scope Cognitively Oriented Curriculum, which evolved from High/Scope's Ypsilanti Perry Preschool Project and the CD Project.

The major differences between PVHS and the other three studies were that 1) PVHS was a national program, which meant that model sponsors provided consultation services but could not participate in the daily operation of the programs; 2) samples assigned to the various models differed greatly on many variables that could be controlled in smaller, local studies; 3) PVHS data provided information on immediate child outcomes only and did not reflect any follow-up information.

The Head Start project shares with the smaller studies the difficulty of obtaining sufficient data on children's aptitude and achievement to permit meaningful statements about the relative effects of curricula. In addition, the vast complexity and size of this project introduced problems generally not faced in intensive local experiments. Problems with control sample selection, instrumentation, and political pressure groups; linkages between experimental sites and project sponsors over distances of hundreds and in some cases thousands of miles; variations in funding levels; status of model development for dissemination (a far different demand on a model than simply implementing it in a single "at home" site or producing professional articles about the theory and training base)—all of these factors conspired with the usual operational problems to make this study extraordinarily difficult to implement. Thus it was not surprising to discover that most models could not be differentiated from their control groups or from each other (Smith, 1973; Weisberg, 1973). However, two clear findings did emerge. The programmed models (such as Engelmann-Becker's DISTAR and Bushell's Behavior Analysis) did achieve significantly higher scores than any of the other models or control groups on academic achievement measures taken at the end of preschool. On aptitude measures at the end of preschool, High/Scope's Cognitively Oriented model evidenced more gains than any other model. As Smith (1973) comments:

> The High/Scope model far outgains any of the other PV models, averaging 23.4 points in 'gains' . . . All of the other PV models gain between 2.5 and 5.2 points, a difference of less than ¼ of a standard deviation in individual test scores . . . In contrast between the observed and the 'observed-expected' gains for the PV and Comparison groups, the High/Scope models stand out as clearly different from all of the others with an advantage favoring the [High/Scope] PV group of roughly 16.5 points. None of the other [models'] measured differences exceeds 3.5 points...there is only one main finding in these data—the High/Scope model *appears to be extraordinarily effective in raising Stanford-Binet scores at least in the short run.* (p. 200; author's italics)

The remaining PV Head Start data are, in general, far less clear—in part, perhaps, because the third year of the project saw a major shift in instrumentation. Several aptitude measures (including the Stanford-Binet) were dropped from the study, and the one that remained, the Preschool Inventory, was greatly altered (Weisberg, 1973). The clearest finding of year three was a repeat of the excellent results obtained in year two by the programmed models in rote recall on the Wide Range Achievement Tests.

## Validity of the CD study

In 1963, Campbell and Stanley advanced the scientific approach to the study of education, in part by proposing two overarching criteria for judging the merits of an educational research study—internal validity and external validity. These terms were defined as follows:

> *Internal validity* is the basic minimum without which any experiment is uninterpretable: Did in fact the experimental treatments make a difference in this specific experimental instance? *External validity* asks the question of *generalizability*: To what populations, settings, treatment variables, and measurement variables can this effect be generalized?

The CD Project is noteworthy among preschool curriculum comparison studies in the strength of its internal validity. Noncurriculum variables (training and supervision of teachers, duration of classroom sessions and home visits, staff/child ratio, and assignment of children to programs) were strictly controlled in order to maintain equivalence in entry Binet scores and family SES. These are some of the major facets of the internal validity of a study. Such objective procedures were seldom possible in the other studies mentioned in the preceding section.

Another aspect of internal validity was mentioned previously: Is measured program impact sufficient to guarantee that an effective program has occurred? In the CD Project, it is evident that each of the programs had a strong impact on children's academic aptitude and achievement.

The external validity of the CD Project is also impressive in some respects. The children appear to be fairly representative of a specific population of children throughout the United States. The measures of academic aptitude and achievement are well standardized and probably are representative of scholastic expectations as well. Even the social ratings collected seem to be generalizable across teacher-raters, despite the typical problems with such measures.

It may be argued that the generalizability of a curriculum is best insured by independent replications of that curriculum in a variety of settings. In that way, variance across replications can be compared to variance across curricula, and one may decide whether there is sufficient consistency across replications of a curriculum to provide *empirical* justification for distinguishing between one curriculum and another. But in curriculum comparison research there is another, perhaps more important, kind of program representativeness: the program implemented should accurately represent its curriculum; if it does not, then the hypotheses concerning the curriculum cannot be tested. Considerable documentation has been presented in this report (see especially chapter III) to demonstrate that the three programs in the CD Project accurately represented three different curricula.

## Key determinants of effective preschool programming

The preschool programs in the CD Project have produced large and sustained impacts on the academic aptitudes of disadvantaged children. We have concluded that the administration and operation of the three programs were key determinants of this success. We believe that an effective preschool program must have a curriculum; a management system that includes training methods and materials for staff; a staff model that guides the relationships of participants as well as their activities; and quality-control procedures to insure that the curriculum, training, and staff model are properly implemented. Each of these components is discussed briefly below from the point of view of the CD Project's experience in successfully implementing three diverse models.

**Curriculum.**  The "content" of a curriculum defines the area of concern and focus of attention; it can range from a single-purpose program that comprises only a portion of the school day (e.g., a reading program) to a set of goals and methods for the entire school day. Curriculum as a whole, though, refers to the process of education (i.e., to all aspects of a model, including parental involvement, cross-age groupings, etc.) and not just to classroom activities.

**Management system.**  An efficient management system is crucial to the success of an educational program, and in order to attain to maximum efficiency, the system must reflect the struggles of a highly dedicated staff. Thus it cannot be preconceived and "applied" but must be "hammered out" in the course of establishing an effective program. The management system will evolve on the basis of decisions taken with respect to the staff/child ratio; staff time for planning and evaluation; identification of necessary equipment and supplies; hiring of support staff; liaison with school officials, local communities, and government agencies; and staff preservice and inservice training.

The nature of the staff training—its content and methods—is probably the most critical of the management variables. We view training as an ongoing process involving all staff for the duration of the project. When a project is in its initial stages, training is often accomplished through an informal method of shared experiences and open communication among staff members. However, for purposes of replication, these shared experiences need to be communicated via audio-visual and written materials.

**Staff model.**  Simply stated, the staff model is the way in which staff members work with one another. Open communication among staff, with each member sharing responsibility, is one important element in a staff model; a positive relationship between staff and those individuals responsible for project decision-making is another. These relationships must be open to be effective. We have found that a hierarchical organizational structure does not produce the quality of staff interaction and program communication that a circular structure does. An effective supervisor must ask key questions, guide staff training activities, and persuade both individual staff members and the group as a whole to face problems of operation they might prefer to ignore. On the whole, the staff model is the key to whether a model "works" at a given site at all stages of the dissemination process.

**Quality-control procedures.**  After the initial training, staff need a system of continuous feedback to insure that the intended model (i.e., the one they were trained in) is in fact the model being implemented. A feedback system that is simple and direct allows staff to change classroom procedures as necessary in order to meet the guidelines prescribed by the model. An observational checklist, for example, with categories drawn from the salient features of the model, may be used for brief periods each week to objectively record the frequencies of various activities in the classroom. Staff can then use the results of these observations to more closely accommodate their actions to the requirements of the model.

An ongoing process of quality control is essential in evaluating the success of any curriculum. First, it permits the outcomes resulting from that particular implementation to be interpreted in terms of the model's characteristics and not confounded by extraneous factors. Second, in cases where evidence exists regarding a model's effectiveness, quality control permits the outcomes of the current implementation to be compared with those of other implementations, because the crucial variable—the model—is held constant.

## Choosing a curriculum

Utilizing standardized measures, it was discovered in the CD Project that three diverse curricula could be equally effective in improving children's academic aptitude and achievement. It has been argued here that the explanation for this success is to be found, not in the curricula themselves, but in the administration and operation of the programs. Given this outcome and this way of explaining it, are we left with any basis for deciding upon a particular model to implement? Clearly this decision rests upon what one values in the *process* of education, and upon what one can reasonably expect to be the *outcome* of such a valuation, for the long term and in the broadest sense of the word.

The CD Project provides information about two important aspects of the process of education: what occurs in the classroom and what occurs in the home. Regarding classroom processes, one's choice of a curriculum would depend on whether one valued such experiences as cooperative play among children, fantasy and imaginative play, individualized teacher-child interactions, competition, extensive opportunities to use materials, praise for mastering new challenges, etc. Observations during the CD Project demonstrated clear curriculum distinctions on these and other dimensions of what children and teachers did in each classroom.

Regarding home processes, the CD Project operated on the assumption that involving parents in their children's learning was crucial to achieving any long-term educational impact. Our longitudinal research and that of others (e.g., Goodson & Hess, 1975) now supports this assumption. Findings on parental participation during CD Project home visits suggest that parents are more involved in educational activities with their children when the program goals are clearly articulated (as in the Language and Cognitive programs). In choosing between several curricula with well articulated goals, one's values about the process of adult-child interaction would come into play. For any given program, differences in parent-child interaction during home learning sessions would parallel those in teacher-child interaction during classroom learning sessions. Thus, in a curriculum like the Language Program, the parent's role would be to directly transmit knowledge and reward the child's performance, whereas in the Cognitive Program, the parent's role would be to facilitate the child's development and foster the child's initiative.

With respect to outcomes broader than traditionally defined educational success, the CD Project can offer only partial information upon which to base the choice of curriculum. If one defines the educational process, that is, how children actually spend their time, as an "outcome" in itself, then observational data from the CD Project show that children in the three programs had very different outcomes by virtue of having very different experiences. The ultimate outcome of any educational experience, however, is the kind of adult which each child becomes. Differential program impact upon adult development is an empirical issue, and one that must await further longitudinal research as individuals progress beyond the school years.

# CONCLUSIONS

Of the three major preschool models compared in the CD Project, all were effective and none was more so than another. This outcome was not anticipated at the start of the project. It was expected that the *academic skills* of children from the Language Program (a "programmed" approach) would be superior to the others, that the general *cognitive abilities* of children from the Cognitive Program (an "open framework" approach) would be greater than the others, and that the *social-emotional abilities* of children from the Unit-Based Program (a "child centered" approach) would be rated higher than the others. While such expectations have been documented in one analysis of National Follow Through evaluation data (Larson, 1977), this has not been the case for either the concurrent or the longitudinal results of the CD Project. On the basis of these results, we have concluded that the principal issue in early childhood education is not *which* curriculum to use but how to manage *any* curriculum to achieve positive results.

The problem of obtaining measurable results in preschool education has plagued the movement for the past decade. However, several recent studies, as well as the present study, have provided support for what has been up to now more a hope than a certainty: that it is possible to affect the lives of children for the good through preschool education (Palmer, 1976; Guinagh and Gordon, 1976; Seitz, Apfel, and Efron, 1976; Weikart, Bond, and McNeil, 1978). It is the particular contribution of the CD Project to have given weight to the idea that the abstractions we call "educational models" are not intrinsically "effective" but become so through the human effort expended in making them real.

The fact that any well delivered curriculum will lead to improved performance on measures of aptitude and achievement in school does not imply, however, that these curricula will lead to other identical ends. When it comes to the question of how best to develop the more global competencies and aptitudes that characterize a productive and rewarding adult life, we confront once again the problem of determining which pedagogical practices are most likely to contribute to these ends. In beginning to address such a formidable issue, educators, social scientists, and policy-makers should consider, first of all, the long-term implications of current alternatives within early childhood education. The actual process of a given curriculum and the long-term outcomes of that curriculum must be understood. Such knowledge will require longitudinal studies that are far more complex than any attempted so far. What hampers our ability to carry out such studies is the lack of instruments sensitive enough to gather the types of data necessary to relate the process and content of early childhood education to adult outcomes. To solve this problem we must develop instruments that will either supplement or replace the familiar standardized tests of the present day.[25] In addition, a comparative study of the life-styles and goals of those adolescents and young adults who participated in different preschool or primary programs may provide some evidence of differential program outcomes.

Secondly, the importance of the family in a child's education must be kept in mind. This is supported by CD Project data showing a difference in school performance favoring CD Project children who had home teaching over those who did not. Parental involvement has been supported by social policy decisions of the past decade and in recent literature reviews (Goodson and Hess, 1975; Bronfenbrenner, 1974), and the CD Project outcomes serve to underscore the importance of such participation in the educational process.

Thirdly, a question raised by a positive but unexpected CD Project finding awaits a definitive answer. The finding was that the youngsters who had been in the three programs maintained their improved IQ scores as they progressed through school—a result which is contrary to the pattern found in all other preschool studies to date. Taken together with the continued success of the children in terms of school achievement (less surprising in light of the longitudinal data from the Perry Project but nonetheless heartening in view of the preponderance of nonsignificant or negative results in this area), this finding brings to the fore the fundamental question raised earlier in this chapter: what made each of these preschool models work so well in this project? In more general terms, as a major research question for the future: what are the parameters of success for any preschool program? Perhaps it is necessary for these parameters to be established empirically before the larger question of the long-term implications of specific educational practices can be addressed.

In summary, the results of the CD Project support these conclusions:

- Preschool education, when effectively delivered, can produce long-term impact on the standardized aptitude and achievement scores of participating children.
- Any of the models represented in this study, if effectively delivered can produce this long-term impact.
- Different models effectively delivered can produce significantly different experiences for participating youngsters, their parents, and staff.

---

[25]See the article, "Alternative Assessment and National Follow Through," by David P. Weikart, in the *High/Scope Report, 1975-76.*

The results of the CD Project leave unanswered two important questions that point the way for further longitudinal research:

- Can different preschool models, effectively delivered, produce significantly different outcomes in the nonacademic areas of children's lives?
- Can different preschool models, effectively delivered, produce significantly different outcomes in the important competencies and satisfactions of adults' lives?

# Appendix A: Procedures for making program comparisons on the PROSE

An observed score n, in one of a group of categories with total score N, may be seen as an estimate of a hypothetical distribution of scores around n. The variance of that distribution combines observer variance and sampling variance. The observer variance around n is indirectly estimated by r, an index of agreement. The index r may be converted to a confidence interval around n, bounded at the bottom by $\hat{n}^-$ and at the top by $\hat{n}^+$. Sampling variance may then be added to this confidence interval by extending its endpoints according to a procedure derived from that of Quesenberry and Hurst (1964).

The index of agreement r used with PROSE categories was based on a procedure suggested by Cartwright (1956). The index r was the percentage of agreement between each simultaneous pair of observations by two observers over four program sessions. It was calculated as follows: $r = a/(a + d)$, the percentage of agreement equals the number of agreements divided by the sum of agreements plus disagreements. Since r was based on the observations of two observers, two observed scores, $2n_r$, were obtained. It is clear, however, that r refers not only to $n_r$, but also to any observed score $n_i$ in the same category. Hence, a and d are obtained scores for the actual calculation of r; but when r refers to a different n, a and d are predicted values, and $r = \hat{a}/(\hat{a} + \dot{d})$.

The predicted number of disagreements $\dot{d}_i$ is a reasonable estimate of the observer confidence interval around $n_i$. Greater confidence may be attached to observations with which another observer agrees than to observations with which another observer disagrees.

It was previously mentioned that two observed scores, $2n_r$, may accompany the calculation of r. Every simultaneous pair of observations that enter into these scores is either one agreement or two disagreements; so $2n_r = 2a + d$. Again, r may refer to $n_i$, so that a and d are predicted values and $2n_i = 2\hat{a} + \dot{d}$. The formula $r = \hat{a}/(\hat{a} + \dot{d})$ may be solved for a. This expression may be substituted for $\hat{a}$ in the previous formula. Then that formula may be solved for $\dot{d}$. This $\dot{d}$ represents the magnitude of the observer confidence interval around $n_i$.

Next, it is necessary to determine the location of $n_i$ within the observer confidence interval $\dot{d}_i$. The lower bound of the observer confidence interval, $\hat{n}^-$, cannot be less than 0. Nor can the upper bound $\hat{n}^+$ exceed N, the total score of all the categories. Both of these situations are avoided if $n_i$ is n/N proportion of the observer confidence interval. So $\hat{n}^- = n - n\dot{d}/N$. The upper bound $\hat{n}^+$ is simply the lower bound plus $\dot{d}$: $\hat{n}^+ = \hat{n}^- + \dot{d}$.

According to a procedure suggested by Quesenberry and Hurst (1964) and modified by Goodman (1965), *sampling* confidence intervals for multinomial proportions within a single population may be obtained. This procedure can be extended to compare categories across two populations by setting a joint alpha level j, such that $1 - j = (1 - \alpha)^2$; solving for j, $j = 1 - (1 - \alpha)^2$. The predicted endpoints of the observer confidence interval, $\hat{n}^-$ and $\hat{n}^+$ may then be substituted for n in the corresponding equations:

$$\hat{\pi}_i^- = \frac{B + 2n^- - \sqrt{B[B + 4n^-(N - n^-)]}}{2(1 + B)}$$

and:

$$\hat{\pi}_i^+ = \frac{B + 2n^+ + \sqrt{B[B + 4n^+(N - n^+)]}}{2(1 + B)}$$

where $\hat{\pi}_i^-$ = the lower bound of the full confidence interval, expressed as a proportion

$\hat{\pi}_i +$ = the upper bound of the full confidence interval, expressed as a proportion

B = the upper j/k times 100th percentile of the chi-square distribution with 1 *df*

and

k = the number of categories

\* \* \* \* \* \* \* \* \* \* \*

## Algebraic derivations of a and d

Given:

$$r = \frac{a}{a + d}$$

Invert:

$$\frac{1}{r} = \frac{a + d}{a}$$

Multiply by a:

$$\frac{a}{r} = a + d$$

Subtract a:

$$\frac{a}{r} - a = d$$

nu

Multiply by r:

$$a - ra = rd$$

Factor out a:

$$a(1 - r) = rd$$

Divide by $(1 - r)$:

$$a = \frac{rd}{1 - r}$$

Given:

$$2n = 2a + d$$

Substitute for a:

$$2n = \frac{2rd}{1 - r} + d$$

Multiply by $(1 - r)$:

$$2n(1 - r) = 2rd + d - rd$$

Perform indicated operations:

$$2n(1 - r) = rd + d$$
$$2n(1 - r) = d(r + 1)$$

Divide by $(r + 1)$:

$$d = \frac{2n(1 - r)}{r + 1}$$

## Frequencies of Observed Events in PROSE Categories

| Category | Program | | |
| --- | --- | --- | --- |
| | Cognitive | Language | Unit-Based |
| Types of Interaction: | 1466 | 1412 | 1436 |
| Child-adult | 457 | 642 | 525 |
| Child-material | 827 | 694 | 730 |
| Child-child | 182 | 76 | 181 |
| Child Toward Adult: | 457 | 642 | 525 |
| Initiates | 56 | 30 | 49 |
| Individual attention | 185 | 86 | 95 |
| In a group | 132 | 414 | 270 |
| Attends to adult | 84 | 112 | 111 |
| Adult Involved: | 453 | 639 | 511 |
| Teacher | 323 | 503 | 480 |
| Adult aide | 92 | 125 | 24 |
| Teenage aide | 38 | 11 | 17 |
| Adult Behavior: | 438 | 632 | 503 |
| Listens, questions | 129 | 84 | 80 |
| Do for child | 16 | 9 | 19 |
| Gives permission | 54 | 5 | 38 |
| Positive feeling | 16 | 7 | 12 |
| Negative feeling | 0 | 8 | 0 |
| Exerts control | 40 | 56 | 22 |
| Tells, explains | 183 | 463 | 332 |
| Attention to Adults: | 455 | 634 | 518 |
| Attentive | 445 | 590 | 504 |
| Inattentive | 10 | 44 | 14 |
| Attention to Materials: | 827 | 694 | 730 |
| Attentive | 662 | 510 | 555 |
| Inattentive | 165 | 184 | 175 |
| Child Toward Peer: | 182 | 76 | 181 |
| Initiates | 84 | 39 | 84 |
| Cooperates | 92 | 34 | 94 |
| Does not cooperate | 6 | 3 | 3 |
| Peer Toward Child: | 178 | 77 | 179 |
| Initiates | 33 | 14 | 22 |
| Cooperates | 133 | 52 | 136 |
| Does not cooperate | 12 | 11 | 21 |
| Mode of Child-Adult Interaction: | 453 | 633 | 514 |
| Verbal | 429 | 617 | 477 |
| Nonverbal | 24 | 16 | 37 |
| Mode of Child-Child Interaction: | 175 | 71 | 174 |
| Verbal | 122 | 34 | 88 |
| Nonverbal | 53 | 37 | 86 |
| Child's Activity Level with Adults: | 456 | 634 | 523 |
| Low | 53 | 239 | 255 |
| Moderate | 403 | 395 | 268 |
| Child's Activity Level with Materials: | 834 | 697 | 740 |
| Low | 128 | 214 | 164 |
| Moderate | 706 | 483 | 576 |
| Child's Activity Level with Children: | 180 | 75 | 181 |
| Low | 6 | 8 | 7 |
| Moderate | 177 | 67 | 174 |
| Nature of Child's Activities: | 1420 | 1384 | 1383 |
| Fantasy | 154 | 9 | 120 |
| Divergent | 233 | 31 | 153 |
| Convergent | 682 | 996 | 786 |
| Work | 137 | 62 | 100 |
| Repetitive | 214 | 286 | 224 |

NOTE: Sums do not always agree across category sets because of missing data.

# Appendix B: Home visit report

PRESCHOOL CURRICULUM DEMONSTRATION PROJECT
1967-68
HOME TEACHING REPORT

```
                                                        L____
                                                        P____
Child's Name_____  Teacher_____  T____

Date of Visit_____  Length of Visit in Minutes____
```

1.  Was the mother in the Home?  Yes____ No____
    If so, give approximate length of time.  ____minutes

2.  Did mother participate in teaching activity <u>in any way</u>?  Yes____ No____
    Is so, give approximate length of time.  ____minutes

3.  Were any adults present other than mother and teacher?  Yes____ No____
    If so, what was their relationship to the child?

    ____father   ____relative   ____teacher's aide   ____guest

4.  Total number of adults in home any time during visit, including
    mother (but not teacher). ____

5.  Total number of children in the home any time during visit, including
    preschool child. _____

6.  Did other children participate in teaching activities?  Yes____ No ____
    If so, approximate length of time other children participated. ____minutes

7.  <u>Conditions Affecting Visit</u>.
    a.  Mother and child ready for teacher?  Yes____ No____
    b.  Prepared place for teacher to work?  Yes____ No____
    c.  Mother found other activities to
        occupy time?                         Yes____ No____

        If yes, what activities_____
        _____
        _____

    d.  Asked specific questions about learning materials, child's
        progress, etc.?                      Yes____ No____

        If yes, number of questions.  1 or 2____  3 or more____

    e.  Mother raises or discusses (undesirable) personal problems
        with teacher?                        Yes____ No____
    f.  List any <u>adverse</u> conditions affecting visit (noise, drinking, etc.)

        _____
        _____
        _____

8.  Indications that teacher's methods, materials, activities, etc.
    were implemented by <u>MOTHER</u> between visits.

    ____bought standard materials

    ____displayed child's work

    ____used materials or helped child with projects left in home

    ____reviewed work with child

    ____introduced complementary activities

    ____initiated teaching of new areas such as words, games, etc.

    ____originated contact with another mother

    ____ other:_____
         _____

9. MOTHER'S reaction to PROGRAM

```
a.  passive   :____:____:____:____:____:____:____:  active
b.  steady    :____:____:____:____:____:____:____:  erratic
c.  open      :____:____:____:____:____:____:____:  closed
d.  hot       :____:____:____:____:____:____:____:  cold
e.  stale     :____:____:____:____:____:____:____:  fresh
f.  inner     :____:____:____:____:____:____:____:  outer
g.  on        :____:____:____:____:____:____:____:  off
h.  empty     :____:____:____:____:____:____:____:  full
i.  smooth    :____:____:____:____:____:____:____:  rough
j.  good      :____:____:____:____:____:____:____:  bad
k.  aimless   :____:____:____:____:____:____:____:  directed
l.  dull      :____:____:____:____:____:____:____:  shiny
m.  grey      :____:____:____:____:____:____:____:  amber
n.  concerned :____:____:____:____:____:____:____:  unconcerned
```

10. MOTHER's relationship with CHILD

```
a.  strict     :____:____:____:____:____:____:____:  permissive
b.  warm       :____:____:____:____:____:____:____:  cold
c.  hard       :____:____:____:____:____:____:____:  soft
d.  passive    :____:____:____:____:____:____:____:  active
e.  steady     :____:____:____:____:____:____:____:  erratic
f.  together   :____:____:____:____:____:____:____:  apart
g.  sweet      :____:____:____:____:____:____:____:  sour
h.  sunny      :____:____:____:____:____:____:____:  cloudy
i.  thick      :____:____:____:____:____:____:____:  thin
j.  good       :____:____:____:____:____:____:____:  bad
k.  aimless    :____:____:____:____:____:____:____:  directed
l.  dull       :____:____:____:____:____:____:____:  shiny
m.  shallow    :____:____:____:____:____:____:____:  deep
n.  helpful    :____:____:____:____:____:____:____:  unhelpful
o.  interested :____:____:____:____:____:____:____:  uninterested
p.  negative   :____:____:____:____:____:____:____:  positive
q.  encouraging:____:____:____:____:____:____:____:  discouraging
r.  concerned  :____:____:____:____:____:____:____:  unconcerned
s.  Unusual response of mother to child either positive or negative:
    _____
    _____
    _____
```

### Mother's Interaction with Child

10a. **Information**

1. Estimate the total amount of information mother communicated to the child.

   very little :____:____:____:____:____:____:____: a great deal

2. Amount of specific information (names of objects, sizes, colors, etc.)

   very little :____:____:____:____:____:____:____: a great deal

3. Amount of general information (concepts, relationships, comparisons, reasons)

   very little :____:____:____:____:____:____:____: a great deal

10b. **Motivation**

1. When mother attempted to motivate the child, did she use negative motivation (threats, punishments)

   very little :____:____:____:____:____:____:____: a great deal

2. positive motivation (rewards, encouragement, positive replies)

   very little :____:____:____:____:____:____:____: a great deal

10c. Feedback Requests

1. To what extent did the mother question the child?

very little :___:___:___:___:___:___:___: a great deal

2. To what extent did the mother <u>ask</u> for specific information? (Ex. What color is this?)

very little :___:___:___:___:___:___:___: a great deal

3. To what extent did the mother <u>ask</u> for general information? (Ex. Why did you do that?)

very little :___:___:___:___:___:___:___: a great deal

4. To what extent did the mother <u>ask</u> the child to do specific things? (Ex. Will you get my shoes?)

very little :___:___:___:___:___:___:___: a great deal

5. To what extent did the mother <u>tell</u> the child to do specific things? (Ex. Turn on light.)

very little :___:___:___:___:___:___:___: a great deal

10d. To what extent did the mother copy your teaching methods?

very little :___:___:___:___:___:___:___: a great deal

11. MOTHER'S relationship with TEACHER

a. warm :___:___:___:___:___:___:___: cool
b. near :___:___:___:___:___:___:___: far
c. open :___:___:___:___:___:___:___: closed
d. fresh :___:___:___:___:___:___:___: stale
e. alive :___:___:___:___:___:___:___: dead
f. sunny :___:___:___:___:___:___:___: cloudy
g. smooth :___:___:___:___:___:___:___: scratchy
h. thick :___:___:___:___:___:___:___: thin
i. good :___:___:___:___:___:___:___: bad
j. aimless :___:___:___:___:___:___:___: directed
k. shallow :___:___:___:___:___:___:___: deep
l. cooperative :___:___:___:___:___:___:___: uncooperative
m. sensitive :___:___:___:___:___:___:___: insensitive
n. talkative :___:___:___:___:___:___:___: hesitant
o. friendly :___:___:___:___:___:___:___: unfriendly

12. <u>Personality Characteristics</u> of Mother (observed by teacher in visit)

a. self-conscious :___:___:___:___:___:___:___: self-assured
b. easily hurt :___:___:___:___:___:___:___: tough-skinned
c. assertive :___:___:___:___:___:___:___: timid
d. domineering :___:___:___:___:___:___:___: self-controlled
e. talkative :___:___:___:___:___:___:___: hesitant
f. confused :___:___:___:___:___:___:___: comprehending
g. restless :___:___:___:___:___:___:___: calm
h. rigid :___:___:___:___:___:___:___: flexible
i. inhibited :___:___:___:___:___:___:___: free
j. conscientious :___:___:___:___:___:___:___: lazy
k. anxious :___:___:___:___:___:___:___: measured
l. preoccupied :___:___:___:___:___:___:___: engrossed
m. indifferent :___:___:___:___:___:___:___: interested
n. rejecting :___:___:___:___:___:___:___: accepting
o. superficial :___:___:___:___:___:___:___: sincere
p. undependable :___:___:___:___:___:___:___: trustworthy
q. distractible :___:___:___:___:___:___:___: attentive
r. friendly :___:___:___:___:___:___:___: unfriendly
s. frank :___:___:___:___:___:___:___: crafty
t. spontaneous :___:___:___:___:___:___:___: constrained
u. responsive :___:___:___:___:___:___:___: oblivious

13. Was there any indication that child used teacher's materials, etc. between visits? Yes_____ No_____

    If yes, indicate below:

    _____child played with materials
    _____worked on project
    _____working with materials when teacher arrived
    _____discussed activities or trips with family
    _____creative play resulting from teacher's intervention

    How do you know this?_____
    _____
    _____
    _____

14. Main educational goal for preschool child.

    _____
    _____
    _____

15. Description of activities with preschool child (Use back of sheet if necessary)

    _____
    _____

16. Child's behavior in program.

    | resistive | :____:____:____:____:____:____:____: | cooperative |
    |-----------|--------------------------------------|-------------|
    | shy | :____:____:____:____:____:____:____: | sociable |
    | withdrawn | :____:____:____:____:____:____:____: | outgoing |
    | anxious | :____:____:____:____:____:____:____: | content |
    | indifferent | :____:____:____:____:____:____:____: | involved |
    | distracted | :____:____:____:____:____:____:____: | diligent |
    | irritable | :____:____:____:____:____:____:____: | cheerful |
    | defensive | :____:____:____:____:____:____:____: | agreeable |
    | passive | :____:____:____:____:____:____:____: | active |
    | stubborn | :____:____:____:____:____:____:____: | persistent |
    | eager | :____:____:____:____:____:____:____: | reluctant |
    | imposing | :____:____:____:____:____:____:____: | compromising |
    | parrotting | :____:____:____:____:____:____:____: | original |
    | talkative | :____:____:____:____:____:____:____: | hesitant |

17. What did the child seem to enjoy most?

    _____
    _____
    _____

18. What did the child enjoy least?

    _____
    _____
    _____

19. Did child request activity? Yes_____ No_____

    In what way did you incorporate the request into the program?

    _____
    _____
    _____

20. What was remembered?_____
    _____

    Not remembered?_____
    _____
    _____

21. Your evaluation of total session.

    _____
    _____

# References

Anastasi, A. *Psychological testing* (3rd. ed.). New York: Macmillan, 1968.

Arthur, G. *The Arthur Adaptation of the Leiter International Performance Scale.* Beverly Hills, Calif.: Psychological Service Center Press, 1952.

Beller, E.K. The evaluation of effects of early educational intervention on intellectual and social development of lower-class disadvantaged children. In E. Grotberg (Ed.), *Critical issues in research related to disadvantaged children.* Princeton, N.J.: Educational Testing Service, 1969.

Bereiter, C., & Engelmann, S. *Teaching disadvantaged children in preschool.* Englewood Cliffs, N.J.: Prentice-Hall, 1966.

Bissell, J.S. *Implementation of planned variation in Head Start.* Washington, D.C.: U.S. Department of Health, Education, and Welfare, Office of Child Development, 1971.

Bloom, B.S. *Stability and change in human characteristics.* New York: John Wiley, 1964.

Bronfenbrenner, U. *A report on longitudinal evaluations of preschool programs: Is early intervention effective?* (Vol. II). Washington, D.C.: U.S. Government Printing Office, 1974. (DHEW Publication No. OHD-75-25)

Campbell, D.T., & Stanley, J.C. Experimental and quasi-experimental designs for research. In N.L. Gage (Ed.), *Handbook of research on teaching.* Chicago: Rand McNally, 1963.

Carroll, J.P. Review of Illinois Test of Psycholinguistics. In O.K. Buros (Ed.), *The seventh mental measurements yearbook* (Vol. 1). New Jersey: Gryphon Press, 1972.

Cartwright, D.S. A rapid non-parametric estimate of multi-judge reliability. *Psychometrika,* 1956, *21*(1), 17-29.

Cronbach, L.J. *Essentials of psychological testing* (2nd ed.). New York: Harper, 1960.

Datta, L., McHale, C., & Mitchell, S. *The effects of the Head Start classroom experience on some aspects of child development: A summary report of national evaluations 1966-1969.* Washington, D.C.: U.S. Government Printing Office, 1976. (DHEW Publication No. OHD-76-30088)

Di Lorenzo, L.T., Salter, R., & Brady, J.J. *Prekindergarten programs for educationally disadvantaged children.* Albany: University of the State of New York, 1969.

Dunn, L.M. *Peabody Picture Vocabulary Test manual.* Circle Pines, Minn.: American Guidance Service, Inc., 1965.

Durost, W.N., Bixler, H.H., Wrightstone, J.W., Prescott, G.A., & Balow, I.H. *Metropolitan Achievement Test manual.* New York: Harcourt, Brace, Jovanovich, Inc., 1971.

Engelmann, S., & Bruner, E.C. *Distar TM reading I.* Science Research Associates, Inc., 1969.

Engelmann, S., & Carnine, D. *Distar TM arithmetic I.* Science Research Associates, Inc., 1969.

Engelmann, S., Osborn, J., & Engelmann, T. *Distar TM language 1.* Science Research Associates, Inc., 1969.

Featherstone, H.J. *Cognitive effects of preschool programs on different types of children.* Cambridge, Mass.: Huron Institute, 1973.

Gehman, I.H., & Matyas, R.P. Stability of the WISC and Binet tests. *Journal of Consulting Psychology,* 1956, *20*, 150-152.

Goodman, L.A. On simultaneous confidence intervals for multinomial proportions. *Technometrics,* 1965, *2*, 2.

Goodson, B.D., & Hess, R.D. *Parents as teachers of young children: An evaluative review of some contemporary concepts and programs.* Palo Alto, Calif.: Stanford University, 1975.

Gray, S.W., & Klaus, R. *The Early Training Project: A seventh-year report.* Nashville, Tenn.: George Peabody College for Teachers, 1969.

Gretzler, A.F. *The use of the Arthur Adaptation of the Leiter International Performance Scale in comparison with the Stanford-Binet Form L-M in diagnosing children with central nervous system dysfunctioning.* Unpublished doctoral dissertation, University of Michigan, 1973.

Guinagh, B.J., & Gordon, I.J. *School performance as a function of early stimulation* (Final Report to Office of Child Development). Gainesville: University of Florida, 1976.

Hawkridge, D., Chalupsky, A., & Roberts, A. *A study of selected exemplary programs for the education of disadvantaged children.* Palo Alto, Calif.: American Institutes for Research in the Behavioral Sciences, 1968.

Hays, W.L. *Statistics for the social sciences.* New York: Holt, Rinehart & Winston, 1963.

Hohmann, M., Banet, B., & Weikart, D.P. *Young children in action: A manual for preschool educators.* Ypsilanti, Mich.: High/Scope Educational Research Foundation, 1978.

Howard, M.J., Hoops, H.R., & McKinnon, A.J. Language abilities of children with differing socioeconomic backgrounds. *Journal of Learning Disabilities,* 1970, *3*(6), 328-335.

Karnes, M.B. *Research and development program on preschool disadvantaged children: Investigations of classroom at-home interventions,* (Vol. I, Final Report). Urbana: University of Illinois, Institute of Research for Exceptional Children, May 1969.

Karnes, M.B. Evaluation and implications of research with young handicapped and low-income children. In J.C. Stanley (Ed.), *Compensatory education for children, ages 2 to 8.* Baltimore, Md.: Johns Hopkins University Press, 1973.

Kennedy, W.A., Van de Reit, V., & White, J.C. A normative sample of intelligence and achievement in negro elementary school children in the southeastern United States. *Monographs of the Society for Research in Child Development,* 1963, *28*(6).

Kirk, S.A., McCarthy, J., & Kirk, W.D. *Examiner's manual: Illinois Test of Psycholinguistic Abilities* (Rev. ed.). Urbana: University of Illinois Press, 1968.

Kohlberg, L., & Mayer, R. Development as the aim of education. *Harvard Educational Review,* 1972, *42,* 449-496.

Larson, J.C. *When program goals and policy questions don't match: An example.* Paper presented at the International Symposium on the Ecology of Care and Education of Children Under Three. Berlin, West Germany: Max-Planck Institute for Educational Research, February 1977.

Leiter, R.G. Manual for the 1948 revision of the Leiter International Performance Scale (Part 1). *Psychology Service Center Journal,* 1959, *11*, 1-72.

Littell, W.M. The Wechsler Intelligence Scale for Children: Review of a decade of research. *Psychological Bulletin,* 1960, *57*, 132-156.

Lukas, C.V., & Wohleb, C. *Implementation of Planned Variation Head Start: 1970-71* (Part 1). Cambridge, Mass.: Huron Institute, 1972.

Maccoby, E.E., & Jacklin, C.N. *The psychology of sex differences.* Menlo Park, Calif.: Stanford University Press, 1974.

McClelland, D., Hiatt, L., Mainwaring, S., & Weathers, T. *The Language Training Curriculum.* Ypsilanti, Mich.: High/Scope Educational Research Foundation, 1970.

McClelland, D., Martin, M., Malte, M., & Richardson, J. *The Unit-Based Curriculum.* Ypsilanti, Mich.: High/Scope Educational Research Foundation, 1970.

McClelland, D., Smith, S., Kluge, J., Hudson, A., & Taylor, C. *The Cognitive Curriculum,* Ypsilanti, Mich.: High/Scope Educational Research Foundation, 1970.

McDaniels, G., Dittman, L., Feldman, M., Fishman, H., Flatter, G., Gardner, A., Gildmeister, J., Goering, J., Green, H., Hunt, J., Matteson, R., Summers, D., Tyler, B., & Urbach, N. *Case studies of children in Head Start Planned Variation, 1970-71.* Washington, D.C.: Department of Health, Education, and Welfare, Office of Child Development, 1972. (DHEW Publication No. OCD-73-1050)

Medley, D.M. *OScAR goes to nursery school: A new technique for recording pupil behavior* (Research Memorandum). Princeton, N.J.: Educational Testing Service, May 1969.

Medley, D.M., Schluck, C.G., & Ames, N.P. *Assessing the learning environment in the classroom: A manual for users of the OScAR 5V* (Research Memorandum 68-9). Princeton, N.J.: Educational Testing Service, 1968a.

Medley, D.M., Schluck, C.G., & Ames, N.P. *Recording individual pupil experiences in the classroom: A manual for PROSE recorders.* Princeton, N.J.: Educational Testing Service, 1968b.

Miller, B., & Dyer, J. Four preschool programs: Their dimensions and effects. *Monographs of the Society for Research in Child Development,* 1975, *40*(162), 5-6.

North, R.D. Review of the California Achievement Tests. In O.K. Buros (Ed.), *The sixth mental measurements yearbook.* New Jersey: Gryphon Press, 1965.

Orgel, A.R., & Dreger, R.M. Comparative study of the Arthur-Leiter and Stanford-Binet Intelligence Scales. *Journal of Genetic Psychology*, 1955, *86*, 359-365.

Palmer, F.H. *The effects of minimal early intervention on subsequent IQ scores and reading achievement, final report for Education Commission of the States*. Stony Brook: State University of New York, 1976.

Paraskevopoulos, J.N., & Kirk, S.A. *The development and psychometric characteristics of the revised Illinois Test of Psycholinguistics*. Urbana: University of Illinois Press, 1969.

Quesenberry, C.P., & Hurst, D.C. Large sample simultaneous confidence intervals for multinomial proportions. *Technometrics*, 1964, *6*, 191-195.

Rivlen, A.M., & Timpane, P.M. (Eds.). *Planned variation in education: Should we give up or try harder?* Washington, D.C.: Brookings Institution, 1975.

Robinson, J.P., Athanasiou, R., & Head, K.B. *Measures of occupational attitudes and occupation characteristics: Appendix A to measures of political attitudes* (draft, 3rd. ed.). Ann Arbor: University of Michigan, Institute for Social Research, 1969.

Rosenberg, L.A., & Stroud, M. Limitations of brief intelligence testing with young children. *Psychological Reports*, 1966, *19*(3, Part 1), 721-722.

Sattler, J.M. *Assessment of children's intelligence*. Philadelphia, Pa.: W.B. Saunders, 1974.

Sears, P.S., & Dowley, E.M. Research on teaching in the nursery school. In N.L. Gage (Ed.), *Handbook of research on teaching*. Chicago: Rand McNally, 1963.

Seifert, K. Comparison of verbal interaction in two preschool programs. *Young Children*, 1969, *24*, 350-355.

Seifert, K. *Preliminary results of observations of three preschool programs* (Research Paper A). Ypsilanti, Mich.: High/Scope Educational Research Foundation, 1970.

Seifert, K. *Preliminary results of observations of teaching style* (Research Paper B). Ypsilanti, Mich.: High/Scope Educational Research Foundation, 1970.

Seitz, V., Apfel, N.H., & Efron, C. *Long-term effects of intervention: A longitudinal investigation*. Connecticut: Hamden-New Haven Cooperative Education Center, 1976.

Severson, R.A., & Guest, K.E. Toward the standardized assessment of the language of disadvantaged children. In F. Williams (Ed.), *Language and poverty: Perspectives on a theme*. Chicago: Markham Publishing, 1970.

Sharp, H.C. A note on the reliability of the Leiter International Performance Scale 1948 revision. *Journal of Consulting Psychology*, 1958, *22*, 320.

Sheriff, F. *Comparison of classroom interactions in three different preschools*. Unpublished doctoral dissertation, University of Michigan, 1971.

Sheriff, F. *Differences in peer interaction among three- and four-year-old children in three different preschool programs* (Research Paper). Ypsilanti, Mich.: High/Scope Educational Research Foundation, 1970.

Smilansky, S. *The effects of sociodramatic play on disadvantaged preschool children*. New York: John Wiley, 1968.

Smith, G., & James, T. The effects of preschool education: Some American and British evidence. *Oxford Review of Education*, 1975, *1*(3), 223-240.

Smith, M.S. *Some short-term effects of project Head Start: A preliminary report on the second year of planned variation, 1970-71*. Cambridge, Mass: Huron Institute, 1973.

Spellacy, F., & Black, F.W. Intelligence assessment in language-impaired children by means of two nonverbal tests. *Journal of Clinical Psychology*, July 1972, *28*(3), 357-358.

Stanford Research Institute. *Implementation of planned variation in Head Start: Preliminary evaluation of planned variation in Head Start according to Follow Through approaches (1969-1970)*. Menlo Park, Calif.: Author, 1971.

Swift, J. Effects of early group experiences: The nursery school and day nursery. In N. Hoffman & L. Hoffman (Eds.), *Review of child development research*. New York: Russell Sage, 1964.

Terman, L.M., & Merrill, M.A. *Measuring intelligence*. Boston: Houghton-Mifflin, 1937.

Terman, L.M., & Merrill, M.A. *Stanford-Binet Intelligence Scale, Form L-M: Manual for the third revision*. Boston: Houghton-Mifflin, 1970.

Tiegs, E.W., & Clark, W.W. *California Achievement Tests: 1957 edition with 1963 norms*. Monterey, Calif.: California Test Bureau, 1963.

Vinter, R.D., Sarri, R.C., Vorwaller, D.J., & Schafer, W.E. *Pupil Behavior Inventory manual.* Ann Arbor, Mich.: Campus Publishers, 1966.

Waddell, K.J., & Cahoon, D.D. Comments on the use of the Illinois Test of Psycholinguistic Abilities with culturally deprived children in the rural south. *Perceptual and Motor Skills,* 1970, *31*, (1), 56-58.

Walker, D.K., Bane, M.J., & Bryk, A. *The quality of the Head Start Planned Variation data* (Vol. 2). Cambridge, Mass.: Huron Institute, 1973.

Wechsler, D. *Wechsler Intelligence Scale for Children.* New York: Psychological Corporation, 1949.

Weikart, D.P. *Preliminary results from a longitudinal study of disadvantaged preschool children.* Paper presented at a convention of the Council for Exceptional Children, St. Louis, Mo., 1967.

Weikart, D.P. Relationship of curriculum, teaching, and learning in preschool education. In J.C. Stanley (Ed.), *Preschool programs for the disadvantaged.* Baltimore, Md.: Johns Hopkins University Press, 1972.

Weikart, D.P. *The Ypsilanti Preschool Curriculum Demonstration Project.* Ypsilanti, Mich.: High/Scope Educational Research Foundation, 1969.

Weikart, D.P., Bond, J.T., & McNeil, J.T. The Ypsilanti Perry Preschool Project: Preschool years and longitudinal results through fourth grade. *Monographs of the High/Scope Educational Research Foundation,* 1978, No. 3.

Weikart, D.P., Deloria, D., Lawser, S., & Wiegerink, R. Longitudinal results of the Ypsilanti Perry Preschool Project. *Monographs of the High/Scope Educational Research Foundation,* 1970, No. 1.

Weikart, D.P. Alternative assessment and national Follow Through. *Report of the High/Scope Educational Research Foundation,* 1975-76, November 1976.

Weikart, D.P., Rogers, L., Adcock, C., & McClelland, D. *The Cognitively Oriented Curriculum: A framework for preschool teachers.* Washington, D.C.: National Association for the Education of Young Children, 1971.

Weisberg, H.I. *Short-term cognitive effects of Head Start programs: A report on the third year of planned variation—1971-72.* Cambridge. Mass.: Huron Institute, 1974.

# COMMENTARY BY J. McV. HUNT
## Professor Emeritus of Psychology & Early Education
## University of Illinois at Urbana-Champaign

It is always interesting to see the final report of an investigation
that one was invited to visit as a consultant at the beginning.
It is always interesting to see how the results correspond with one's
expectations and especially interesting if they come out in ways
contrary to one's expectations and contrary to what one would
expect to be the vested interests of the investigator.

The purpose of the Curriculum Demonstration Project has
been to determine which of the three main kinds of curricula preva-
lent in the compensatory education of the 1960s is most effective.
Weikart and his staff have attempted to conduct a genuine experiment
in which only curriculum-specific factors vary significantly.

So much time is required for such investigations, even if only
the short-range permanence of effects are to be assessed, that it
is now nine years since David Weikart invited me to Ypsilanti as one
of his group of outside consultants. I was impressed then with
the acceptance of Weikart and his staff of the substantially greater
first-year gains in IQ from the Bereiter-Engelmann programmed
curriculum. I noted not even a rueful comment such as might be
expected from pride in the Piaget-inspired open framework
curriculum they had devised. As it turns out, by the end of the fourth
grade, the gains from the three curricula, even though still substantial enough to be educationally significant, have largely equalized.
No longer do they differ significantly. This finding puzzles
me. My own research and that of others working with children under
three years has been turning up an unexpected amount of specificity
between kinds of experience and kinds of developmental advance.
An expected sort of specificity does show during the first year;
the programmed curriculum pushes the children in it well
ahead of others in language skill, which accounts for the increase in
IQ. But why do these children fail to maintain their lead? I am
inclined to guess that greater opportunity for children to choose and
to start their own activities in the freer curricula may foster a
self-winding initiative which enables them to achieve on their own
the language skills actively taught to those in the programmed
curriculum. But this is a guess, hopefully an educated one based on
findings in other areas of research, but still only a guess. I find no
evidence from other measures used in this study to substantiate or
deny it. Moreover, until we develop useful measures of such
characteristics as initiative, we can have nothing but guessed
answers to such questions.

Nine years ago I wondered whether any of these curricula could capture enough of the intimate, proximal experience of these children in 2.5 hours a day to make anything but a temporary boost in the achievement of academic skills. It is highly gratifying to find that all three of them result in gains which are substantial enough to be educationally significant, substantial enough to enable nearly all of these children, all of whom were at risk for the expensive programs in special education, to escape them. Moreover, the effects do endure through the fourth grade. Since most other programs have been less successful, I wonder why. Again I must guess, but three factors seem to be important. Since the duration of experience is regularly found to be an important factor in how long its effects last, I suspect that having children in these curricula for two years is crucial. Since the home is typically more important than a school whch has children for only 2.5 hours a day, as Christopher Jencks has documented in his *Inequality,* I suspect that the second most important factor is the involvement of the parents in concern for the educational process. Finally, since many Head Start programs failed for want of effective delivery of the educational experiences, I suspect it was the administrative encouragement of staff commitment to the teaching and the techniques of quality control which accounted for effective delivery in this demonstration project.

J. McVicker Hunt
University of Illinois
April 13, 1978